photographic lighting

essential skills

photographic lighting

fourth edition

john child

mark galer

AMSTERDAM • BOSTON • HEIDELBERG • LONDON • NEW YORK • OXFORD
PARIS • SAN DIEGO • SAN FRANCISCO • SINGAPORE • SYDNEY • TOKYO
Focal Press is an imprint of Elsevier

Focal Press is an imprint of Elsevier
The Boulevard, Langford Lane, Kidlington, Oxford OX5 1GB, U
30 Corporate Drive, Suite 400, Burlington, MA 01803, USA

First published 1999
Reprinted 2000
Second Edition 2002
Reprinted 2003
Third Edition 2005
Fouth Edition 2008
Reprinted 2009

British Library Cataloguing in Publication Data
A catalogue record for this book is available from the British Library

Library of Congress Cataloguing in Publication Data
A catalogue record for this book is available from the Library of Congress

ISBN: 978-0-240-52095-7

For more information on all Focal Press publications visit our website at:

www.elsevierdirect.com

Printed and bound in China
09 10 11 11 10 9 8 7 6 5 4 3 2

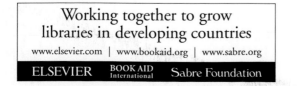

Working together to grow
libraries in developing countries

www.elsevier.com | www.bookaid.org | www.sabre.org

ELSEVIER   BOOK AID International   Sabre Foundation

Acknowledgements

Among the many people who have helped make this book possible, we wish to express our thanks to the following:

~ Michael E. Stern for his technical review and contribution to content.
~ Michael Wennrich, Les Horvat and John Hay for their continuing support.
~ The students of RMIT University, Melbourne for their illustrative input, enthusiasm and friendship.
~ Our families for their love, encouragement and understanding.

Picture credits

Ansel Adams (CORBIS/Ansel Adams Publishing Trust); Spiro Alexopoulos; Paul Allister; Tim Barker; Kata Bayer; Shane Bell; Rodrick Bond; Andrew Boyle; Nigel Carboon; Mick Downes; Samantha Everton; Joanne Gamvros; Martina Gemmola; Wil Gleeson; Andrew Goldie; Shaun Guest; Tracey Hayes; Orien Harvey; John Hay; Paulina Hyrniewiecka; Itti Karuson; Tommy Kellner; Jana Liebenstein; Line Mollerhaug; Chris Mollison; James Newman; Matthew Orchard; Martin Reftel; Martin Ryner; Fabio Sarraff; Craig Shell; Amelia Soegijono; Hayley Sparks; Tim Stammers; Michael E. Stern; Daniel Tückmantel; Shivani Tyagi; Rebecca Umlauf; Victoria Verdon Roe; Charanjeet Wadwha; Michael Wennrich; Daniel Willmott; Stuart Wilson.

Cover image by Daniel Tückmantel.
Technical illustrations (photographic) by Jana Liebenstein, Dianna Snape and Charanjeet Wadwha.
Illustrations by Mark Galer.
All other photographs are by the authors or from the RMIT Alumni Collection.

Contents

skill ac

Contents

Contents

Contents

Samantha Everton

acquisition module>>

quisition

Introduction

Lighting is the essential skill in photography. From the captured image of a fleeting moment using existing light to the highly structured and preconceived advertising image using introduced lighting. To understand and improve these skills this book deals with working on location, primarily using the existing light source, and in the studio using artificial light sources. The information, activities and assignments provide the essential techniques for creative and competent photography. The study guides offer a comprehensive and highly structured learning approach, giving both support and guidance in a logical and sequential manner. Basic theoretical information is included with an emphasis on practical advice that will maximize the opportunities for creative photography.

Rodrick Bond

Acquisition of technique

This book is designed to help you learn the technical and creative aspects of photography. The initial chapters provide the framework for the assignment briefs; the other chapters will help you acquire the skills required to confidently undertake a broad range of lighting situations. Terminology is kept as simple as possible using only those terms in common usage. Emphasis has been placed upon a practical approach to the subject and the application of the essential skills.

Application of technique

The book concludes with several chapters devoted to the practical application of the skills acquired. Assignments can be undertaken allowing the photographer to express themselves and their ideas through the appropriate application of design and technique. This book offers a structured learning approach that will give the photographer a framework and solid foundation for working independently and confidently in a studio or on location.

The essential skills

The essential skills required to become a professional photographer take time and motivation. Skills should be practised repeatedly so they become practical working knowledge rather than basic understanding. Practice the skills obtained in one chapter and apply them to each of the following activities or assignments. Eventually the technical and creative skills can be applied intuitively or instinctively and you will be able to communicate with clarity and creativity.

Process and progress

This book is intended as an introduction to location and studio photography. The emphasis has been placed upon a practical approach to the application of essential skills. The activities and assignments cover a broad range and it is possible to achieve acceptable results without the need for large amounts of expensive equipment.

A structured learning approach

The study guides contained in this book offer a structured learning approach forming the framework for working with photographic lighting and the essential skills for personal creativity and communication. They are intended as an independent learning source to help build design skills, including the ability to research, plan and execute work in a systematic manner. Adoption of a thematic approach is encouraged, recording all research and activities in the form of a Visual Diary and Record Book.

Flexibility and motivation

The assignments contain a degree of flexibility, and allow for the choice of subject matter. This encourages the pursuit of individual interests whilst still directing work towards answering specific criteria. This approach allows the maximum opportunity to develop self-motivation. Emphasis is placed on image design, communication of content and the essential techniques required for competent and consistent image capture and creation. The practical problems of contrast are discussed and additional lighting in the form of flash and tungsten is introduced. Activities and assignments should be undertaken to encourage expression of ideas through the appropriate application of design and technique. Demonstration of skills learnt in preceding study guides is a desirable criteria whenever appropriate.

Implementation of the curriculum

This book provides a suitable adjunct to *Essential Skills: Studio Photography*, *Essential Skills: Digital Photography in Available Light* and *Essential Skills: Photoshop*.

Website

A dedicated website exists to assist with the use of this book. Revision exercises are included on the site as are numerous links and up to date advice and references. The revision exercises should be viewed as another activity which the user resources and completes independently. This will encourage the demonstration of the skills and knowledge acquired in the process of working through the activities and revision exercises by completion of a self-directed series of projects and assignments in the books *Essential Skills: Studio Photography* and *Essential Skills: Digital Photography on Location*. The address for the website is: www.photographyessentialskills.com

Independent learning

The study guides are designed to help you learn both the technical and creative aspects of photography. You will be asked to complete various tasks including research activities, revision activities and practical assignments. The information and experience you gain will provide you with a framework for all your future photographic work.

Activities and assignments

By completing all the activities, assignments and revision exercises you will learn how other images were created, how to create your own and how to communicate visually. The images you produce will be a means of expressing your ideas and recording your observations. Photography is a process best learnt in a series of steps. Once you apply these steps you will learn how to be creative and produce effective images. The study guides also explain many of the key issues which are confusing and often misunderstood - an understanding of which will reinforce and facilitate creative expression.

Using the study guides

The study guides have been designed to give you support during your photographic learning. On the first page of each is a list of aims and objectives identifying the skills covered and how they can be achieved. The activities are to be started only after you have first read and understood the supporting section on the preceding pages. At the end of each chapter the relevant revision exercise from the supporting website should be undertaken to determine the extent to which the information has been assimilated. After completion of the activities and revision exercises the 'Assignments' should be undertaken.

Equipment needed

The course has been designed to teach you photographic lighting with the minimum amount of equipment. You will need a camera with manual controls or manual override. However, large amounts of expensive equipment are not necessary to gain an understanding of the use of light. Observation of daylight, ambient light, normal household light globes, desk lamps, outdoor lighting, torches and small flash units can be adapted and utilized to produce acceptable results. Supplemented with various reflectors (mirrors, foil, white card) and assorted diffusion material (netting, cheesecloth, tracing paper, Perspex) a degree of lighting control can be achieved. Many of the best photographs have been taken with very simple equipment. Photography is more about understanding and observing light, and then recreating lighting situations to achieve form, perspective and contrast when working with a two-dimensional medium.

Gallery

At the end of each study guide is a collection of work produced with varying combinations of daylight, ambient light, flash and tungsten light sources.

Research and resources

To gain the maximum benefit from each assignment use the activities contained in the study guide as a starting point for your research. You will only realize your full creative potential by looking at a variety of images from different sources. Artists and designers find inspiration for their work in different ways, but most find that they are influenced by other people's work they have seen and admired. Furthermore, it is essential that anyone undertaking any creative endeavor has some understanding of the context of their art. Researching relevant artists and practitioners is an essential element of this process.

Getting started

Collect images relevant to the activity you have been asked to complete. This collection of images will act as valuable resource for your future work. Do not limit your search to photographs. Explore all forms of the visual arts. By using elements of different images you are not copying but using the information as inspiration for your own creative output. Talking through ideas with friends, family, or anyone willing to listen will help you clarify your thinking and develop your ideas.

Daniel Tückmantel

Choosing resources

When looking for images, be selective. Use only high quality sources. Not all photographs are well designed or appropriate. Good sources may include high quality magazines and journals, photographic books, exhibitions and the web. You may have to try many various sources to find suitable material. In addition, be aware of exhibitions coming to your local galleries.

Visual Diary

A Visual Diary is a record of all visual and written stimuli influencing or forming the basis of an idea for the photographic assignments and practical work to be completed.

In its most basic form this could be a scrapbook full of tear sheets (examples) and personal scribbles. It would, however, be of far more value if your Visual Diary contained more detail relating to an increasing awareness of your visual development in discriminating between good and bad examples of location and studio lighting. This should include design, composition, form and light applicable to any visual art form.

Joanne Gamvros

The Visual Diary should contain:

- A collection of work by photographers, artists, writers, filmmakers relevant to your photographic studies.
- Website addresses and links.
- Sketches of ideas for photographs.
- A collection of images illustrating specific lighting and camera techniques.
- Brief written notes supporting each entry in the diary.

Record Book

The Record Book forms the documented evidence of the practical considerations and outcomes associated with the completion of each activity and assignment. It should contain comprehensive information enabling the photographer to reproduce an identical image at another time and/or place. This is common professional practice.

Ball

	26/08/07
Camera	Nikon D70
ISO	100
Lighting ratio	Spotlight f64
	Floodlight f45
	Reflector f32
Meter reading	Incident 2 seconds f45
Polaroid exposure	3 seconds f45
Exposure	3 seconds f45
Process	Normal

Spotlight from back to create rim light. Floodlight from left, centre of light at point where front of ball falls into shadow. Creates gradual decrease in light across front. White reflector to right side of ball.

The Record Book should contain:

- ~ An information sheet for each activity and assignment.
- ~ Technical requirements and equipment used.
- ~ Lighting diagram, camera to subject diagram, camera angle and height (measurements and specifications).
- ~ Meter readings of light ratios and exposure.
- ~ ISO and color balance.
- ~ All digital files used to reach the final result.
- ~ Props (use and source) and any other information relevant to each photograph.

Research, presentation and storage

Research

With each assignment you should provide evidence of how you have developed your ideas and perfected the techniques you have been using. This should be presented in an organized way showing the creative and technical development of the finished piece of work. Make brief comments about images that have influenced your work. Photocopy these images and include them with your research.

Presentation

Presentation can have a major influence on how your work is viewed.

- When presenting on-screen make sure the software and computer are compatible.
- Ensure that all of your digital images are cropped neatly.
- Mount all printed work neatly and label appropriately.
- Ensure that horizontal and/or vertical elements are corrected if this is appropriate (sloping horizon lines are visually unnerving to look at).

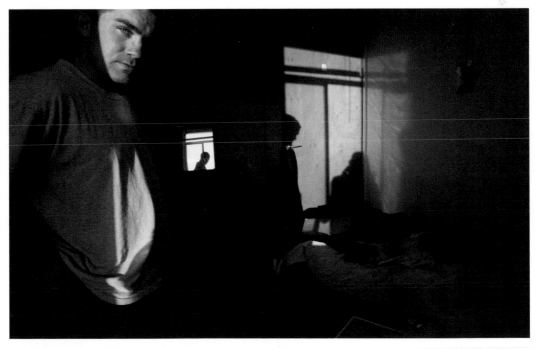

Orien Harvey

Storage

It is best to standardize your final portfolio so that it has an overall 'look' and style.

- Assignments should be kept in a folder slightly larger than your mounted work.
- Analog material if used should be stored in a dust and moisture-free environment.
- Digital files should be burned to a CD, saved to a portable disk or hard drive or an online storage site.

Rodrick Bond

characteristics of light

Mark Galer

essential skills

~ An understanding of how light changes the character and mood of an image.

~ An awareness of subject contrast and its effect upon film or image sensors.

~ Developing the skills to control introduced lighting on location and in the studio.

~ Creating images demonstrating how lighting techniques control communication.

~ Documenting the progress and development of your ideas.

Introduction

Light is the essence of photography. Without light there is no photography. Light is the photographer's medium. The word photography is derived from the ancient Greek words, 'photos' and 'graph', meaning 'light writing'. To understand light the photographer must be fully conversant with its qualities and behavior. In mastering the medium the photographer learns to take control over the creation of the final image. This takes knowledge, skill and craftsmanship. It can at first seem complex and sometimes confusing. However, with increased awareness and practical experience light becomes an invaluable tool to communication.

Seeing light

In order to manage a light source, we must first be aware of its presence. Often our preoccupation with content and framing can make us oblivious to the light falling on the subject and background. We naturally take light for granted. This can sometimes cause us to simply forget to 'see' the light. When light falls on a subject it creates a range of tones we can group into three main categories: Highlights, Mid-tones and Shadows.

Each of these can be described by their level of illumination (how bright, how dark) and their distribution within the frame. These are in turn dictated by the relative position of Subject, Light source and Camera.

Image 1 - Shivani Tyagi

Image 2 - Rebecca Umlauf

Activity 1

Describe the above images in terms of highlights, mid-tones and shadows.
Draw diagrams to indicate the relative position of subject, light source and camera.

Introducing light

The major difference between studio and location photography is the studio itself has no ambient or inherent light. The photographer starts with no light at all and has to previsualize how to light the subject matter and what effect that light will have upon the subject. Studio photographers have to conceive the lighting of the subject rather than observe what already exists. This requires knowledge, craft, observation, organization and discipline. Good studio photography takes time, lots of time, and **patience**.

Mark Galer

Understanding the nature of light

In order to make the best use of an artificial light source, we must first be aware of how light acts and reacts in nature. Observation of direct sunlight, diffuse sunlight through cloud and all its many variations will develop an understanding of the two main artificial studio light sources available. A spotlight (point light source) imitates the type of light we see from direct sunlight, a hard light with strong shadows and extreme contrast. A floodlight (diffuse light source) imitates the type of light we see on an overcast day, a soft diffuse light with minor variations in contrast and few shadows.

To understand light fully it is essential to examine its individual characteristics.

- Source
- Intensity
- Quality
- Direction
- Contrast
- Color.

Source
Ambient
Ambient light is existing natural or artificial light present in any environment. Ambient light can be subdivided into four major categories:

- Daylight
- Tungsten
- Fluorescent
- Firelight.

Daylight
Daylight is a mixture of sunlight and skylight. Sunlight is the dominant or main light. It is warm in color and creates highlights and shadows. Skylight is the secondary light. It is cool in color and fills the entire scene with soft diffused light. Without the action of skylight, shadows would be black and detail would not be visible. White balance is usually calibrated to daylight at noon (5500K). When images are recorded at this time of the day the colors and tones reproduce with neutral values, i.e. neither warm nor cool.

Tungsten
A common type of electric light such as household bulbs/globes and photographic lamps. A tungsten element heats up and emits light. Tungsten light produces very warm tones when used as the primary light source. Underexposure occurs due to the lack of blue light in the spectrum emitted. Digital cameras can be set to automatically adjust the white balance to correct the color cast from light sources of different color temperatures or this can be set by the photographer by choosing either a white balance setting or creating a customized white balance setting (see Color Correction and Filtration > Color accuracy in camera).

Fluorescent
Phosphors inside fluorescent tubes radiate light after first absorbing ultraviolet light from mercury vapor emission. The resulting light from most fluorescent tubes produces a strong green cast that can be difficult to correct and is not apparent to the human vision. If used as a primary light source the results are often unacceptable due to the broad flat light and the strong color cast. Daylight balanced fluorescent tubes and compact fluorescent lamps or CFLs are available and these are increasingly being used as a photographic light source (see Lighting on Location > Halogen or daylight balanced fluorescent lamps on location).

Firelight
Light from naked flames can be very low in intensity. With very long exposures it can be used to create atmosphere and mood with its rich red tones.

Artificial light

Tungsten (non-domestic)

There are many variations of non-domestic tungsten light sources used in photographic, film and TV studios. They all fall in to two major categories, floodlight and spotlight. The majority have a color temperature of 3200 – 3400K. A simple floodlight would have an output of 500 watts and a basic focusing spotlight around 650 watts. Professional spotlights come with barn doors and nets. Barn doors are metal flaps used to control the shape and quantity of light falling on the subject. Nets are pieces of wire gauze of varying densities that reduce the quantity and alter the quality of the light by diffusing the light at its source. Similar items used to create the same effect when using a floodlight are known as cutters (shape and quantity) and various diffusion material (quantity and quality). See 'Studio Lighting'.

Rodrick Bond

Flash (studio)

The main differences between location and studio-based flash are size, cost and output. Studio flash is physically larger, costs a great deal more and produces a far greater output of light. The precise color temperature between different flash units may vary but the majority have a color temperature similar to daylight (5500 – 7000K). Despite the names, swimming pool, soft box, fish fryer, honeycomb etc., these are really only large or smaller versions of a diffuse light source. The use of an open flash (direct light to subject without diffusion) will give a similar effect to a spotlight. Most brands have focusing capabilities and the range of attachments available for tungsten exist in one form or another for use with flash. See 'Studio Lighting'.

Activity 2

Research the cost and availability of photographic light sources (tungsten and flash), stands and associated equipment. Research any low cost lighting alternatives not specifically designed for photographic needs. Compare their output, measured in watts, and cost.

Intensity

Light intensity is a description of the level of a light's brightness. The intensity of light falling on a subject can be measured using a light meter. This is called an 'incident reading'. A light meter built into a camera does not directly measure the intensity of light falling on the subject but the level of light reflected from it. This is called a 'reflected reading'.

Mark Galer

Reflectance

Regardless of the intensity of the light falling on the subject different levels of light will be reflected from the subject. The amount of light reflecting from a surface is called 'subject reflectance'. The levels of reflectance vary according to the color, texture and angle of the light to the subject. A white shirt will reflect more light than a black dress. A sheet of rusty metal will reflect less light than a mirror. In all cases the level of reflectance is directly proportional to the viewpoint of the camera. If the viewpoint of the camera is equal to the angle of the light to the subject the reflectance level will be greater. The level of reflected light is therefore determined by:

- ~ Reflectance of the subject.
- ~ Intensity of the light source.
- ~ Angle of viewpoint and light to subject.
- ~ Distance of the light source from the subject.

Although the intensity of the light source may remain constant (such as on a sunny day) the level of reflected light may vary.

Fall-off

As the distance between the subject and the light source increases the level of light illuminating the subject decreases. The amount of light falling on a subject decreases to 25% of its original intensity when the light to subject distance is doubled. This change in the level of illumination is called fall-off and is quantified by the 'Inverse square law' (observe the fall-off in the image below).

For example, if a reading of f16 is obtained when the light to subject distance is one metre, at two metres the reading would be f8, at four metres f4. These rules do not change regardless of the light source. Although fall-off does not present a problem when working with direct sunlight (all subjects being the same distance from the sun), it does need to be considered with reflected light, window light and artificial light sources. The visual effect of subjects at differing distances to the light source is uneven illumination.

Inverse square law

When a surface is illuminated by a point source of light the intensity of the light at the surface is inversely proportional to the square of its distance from the light source.

Daniel Tückmantel

Activity 3

Using a floodlight or window light, illuminate two people standing at one and two metres from the light source.

Position the people two metres further away from the light source so that the people are now three and four metres from the light source.

Does the difference in brightness between the two people illuminated by the light source increase or diminish as the light source moves further away from the subjects?

Quality

Light from a point light source such as an open flash or the sun is described as having a 'hard quality'. The directional shadows created by this type of light are dark with well-defined edges. The shadows created by the sun are dark but not totally devoid of illumination. This illumination is provided by reflected skylight. The earth's atmosphere scatters some of the shorter blue wavelengths of light and provides an umbrella of low-level light. Artificial point light sources create a much harsher light when used at night or away from the softening effects of skylight. The light from a point light source can also be diffused, spread or reflected off larger surface areas. Directional light maintains its 'hard quality' when reflected off a mirror surface but is scattered in different directions when reflected off a matte surface. This lowers the harshness of the light and the shadows now receive proportionally more light when compared to the highlights. The light is said to have a softer quality. The shadows are less dark (detail can be seen in them) and the edges are no longer clearly defined.

Harsh light   *Soft light - Orien Harvey*

The smaller the light source, the harder the light appears.
The larger the light source, the softer the light appears.

The control over quality of light is an essential skill when on location. Often the photographer will encounter scenes where the quality of the available light creates enormous difficulties for the latitude of the image sensor. The photographer must learn techniques to alter the quality of light or risk loss of detail and information. The quality of light, whether hard or soft, can be changed by diffusion and reflection.

Diffusion

A light source can be diffused by placing certain materials between the light source and the subject. This has the affect of diffusing and spreading the light over a greater area by artificially increasing the size of the source. Relative to its size, the further the diffusion material from the light source the larger the light appears to be. This softens the shadows, increases shadow detail and decreases the measured amount of light falling on the subject.

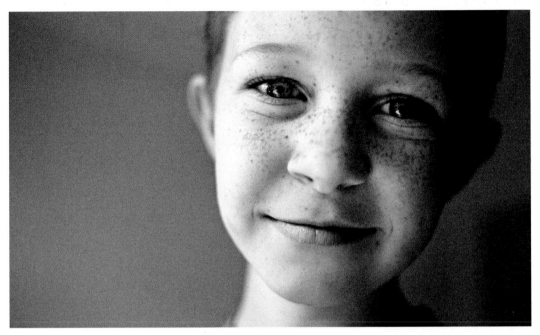

Rodrick Bond

Reflection

Light is reflected off surfaces to varying degrees. More light will be reflected off silver than off black. Reflection is a simple way of changing the quality of light. The amount of light reflected off a surface is directly related to subject contrast. A point source of light will give hard shadows to the left side of a subject when lit from the right. This is called high contrast as there are only highlights and shadows. A reflector used to reflect the light passing the subject back onto the left side would reduce the contrast by raising the detail in the shadows to a level closer to the highlights.

Activity 4

Illuminate a subject with a range of tones (another person) under many varied light sources. Include daylight, domestic lighting, street lighting, commercial and industrial lighting and light sources in your studio.
Observe how the quality of the light varies from light source to light source and the differences in the reflective levels of elements in the photographs.
Modify the quality of a light source by placing a diffusing material between the light source and the subject. Observe the differences in the highlights and shadows.

Direction
In the studio

The direction of light determines where shadows fall and their source can be described by their relative position to the subject. Shadows create texture, shape, form and perspective. Without shadows photographs can appear flat and visually dull. A subject lit from one side or behind will not only separate the subject from its background but also give it dimension. A front lit subject may disappear into the background and lack form or texture. In nature the most interesting and dramatic lighting occurs early and late in the day. Observing and adapting these situations is a starting point to studio lighting.

Mark Galer

On location

Many location photographs look flat and uninteresting. Photographers arriving at a location when the sun is high find a flat, even illumination to the environment. The colors can look washed out and there is little or no light and shade to create modelling and texture. The mood and atmosphere of a location can be greatly enhanced by the realization that most successful location images are taken when the sun is low, dawn or dusk, or as it breaks through cloud cover to give uneven and directional illumination. When the sun is high or diffused by cloud cover the mood and the subject contrast usually remain constant. When the sun is low the photographer can often choose a variety of moods by controlling the quantity, quality and position of shadows within the image. Colors are often rich and intense and morning mists can increase the mood dramatically.

Contrast

Contrast is the degree of difference between the lightest and darkest tones of the subject or photographic image. A high-contrast photograph is one where dark tones and bright tones dominate over the mid-tones within the image. The highest contrast image possible is one containing only two tones, black and white, and where no mid-tones remain. A low-contrast image is one where mid-tones dominate the image and there are few if any tones approaching white or black.

Without contrast photographic images would appear dull and flat. It is contrast within the image that gives dimension, shape and form. Awareness and the ability to understand and control contrast is an essential skill to work successfully in the varied and complex lighting situations that arise on location and in the studio.

High contrast - Kata Bayer   *Low contrast - Tracey Hayes*

Affecting contrast

Contrast is affected by the difference in the intensity of light falling on a subject and the intensity this light reflects back to the viewer or light-sensitive surface. Light usually strikes three-dimensional subjects unevenly. Surfaces facing the light receive full illumination, whilst surfaces turned away from the light receive little or none. Different surfaces reflect different amounts of light. A white shirt reflects more light than black jeans. The greater the difference in the amount of light reflected, the greater the subject contrast. When harsh directional light illuminates a subject overall contrast increases. The highlight tones facing the light source continue to reflect a high percentage of the light whilst the dark tones in the shadows may reflect little. The difference between the darkest and the lightest tone increases, leading to increased contrast.

Limitations of the medium

The human eye can register detail in a wide range of tones simultaneously. Film and digital image sensors are unable to do this. They can record only a small range of what human vision is capable of seeing. The photographer has the option of recording a selected range of tones or seeking ways of lowering the contrast. In an attempt to visualize how the contrast of a subject will be translated by the photographic medium many photographers use the technique of squinting or narrowing the eyes to view the scene. Squinting removes detail from shadows and makes the highlights stand out. In this way it is possible to estimate the contrast of the resulting image.

Contrast on location

Cloud cover diffuses the light leading to lower contrast images. Shadows appear less harsh and with softer edges. The lighting may be described as being flat and the film or digital image sensor will usually be able to record the range of tones present if accurately exposed. When direct sunlight strikes the subject the contrast usually exceeds the film or image sensor's capability to record the range of tones. The photographer may have to seek a compromise exposure.

Kata Bayer

Creating contrast

Working in a studio situation where the subject and lighting are under the control of the photographer, contrast is usually by design rather than by any error of judgement. As all the elements that cause contrast are controlled by the photographer it can be created and used to great effect. Placing highlights in shadow areas and deep shadows through mid-tones can create interesting images.

Color

The visible spectrum of light consists of a range of wavelengths from 400 nanometres (nm) to 700nm. Below 400nm is UV radiation and X-rays and above 700nm is infrared (all capable of being recorded photographically). When the visible spectrum is viewed simultaneously we see 'white light'. This broad spectrum of colors creating white light can be divided into the three primary colors: red, green and blue. The precise mixture of primary colors in white light may vary from different sources. The light is described as cool when predominantly blue, and warm when predominantly red. Human vision adapts to different mixes of white light and will not pick up the fact a light source may be cool or warm unless compared directly with another in the same location.

The light from tungsten bulbs and firelight consists predominantly of light towards the red end of the spectrum. The light from tungsten lamps is also predominantly light towards the red end of the spectrum. The light from flash consists predominantly of light towards the blue end of the spectrum. Daylight is a mixture of cool skylight and warm sunlight. Image sensors balanced to 'Daylight' will give fairly neutral tones with noon summer sunlight. When the direct sunlight is obscured or diffused, however, the skylight can dominate and the tones record with a blue cast. As the sun gets lower in the sky the light gets progressively warmer and the tones will record with a yellow or orange cast. The color of light is measured by color temperature, usually described in terms of degrees Kelvin (K). This scale refers to a color's visual appearance (red - warm, blue - cold).

Color correction

When using a digital camera and saving to JPEG or TIFF color correction is achieved by adjusting the white balance to the dominant light source. Alternatively save to the Camera Raw format and assign the white balance in post-production.

Note > To achieve color consistency it is recommended to use a 'Custom' white balance or white balance preset rather than the 'Auto' white balance setting. When using Auto white balance small variations of subject color, rather than changes in the color temperature of the light source, can also lead to variations in the white balance selected by the camera.

Activity 5

Experiment by using a warm colored filter over a flash unit to capture a room lit with tungsten light (be sure to use an exposure that will record the available light present, e.g. a 'slow sync' flash setting). Take a second image without using the filter and compare the results.

Color correction - Raw

All digital cameras capture in Raw but only the medium- to high-end cameras offer the user the option of saving the images in this Raw format. Selecting the Raw format in the camera stops the camera from processing the color data collected from the sensor when each image is captured. Digital cameras typically process the sensor's color data by applying the white balance, sharpening and contrast settings set by the user in the camera's menus. Selecting the Raw format prevents this image processing taking place. The Raw data is what the sensor 'saw' before the camera processes the image and many photographers have started to refer to, and use, this file as the 'digital negative'.

Working with a Camera Raw editor

To harness the full power and functionality of the Raw format, a dedicated Raw editor is required. Whilst many stand-alone versions of such software are available, Adobe released a plug-in (known as Adobe Camera Raw) for Photoshop 7 back in 2003 and it is now fully integrated into all versions of Photoshop. To retain the white balance setting as originally selected in the camera at the time of capture, click the 'As Shot' option in the software used to edit your Raw images. However, if it is felt that changes need to be made to these parameters, they can easily be achieved by use of the 'Temperature' and 'Tint' sliders. In particular, moving the Temperature slider to the left shifts the colors to the blue end of the spectrum to compensate for a yellowish cast resulting from an image created with a light source of low color temperature. Similarly moving the slider to the right will compensate for a high original color temperature by adjusting the image in the yellow direction. The Tint slider enables further fine-tuning in the green/magenta directions, which are most commonly needed for images captured under fluorescent lighting environments.

Maintaining color accuracy across multiple devices

Have you ever walked into a TV shop or the cabin of an aircraft and noticed that all the screens are all showing the exactly the same TV program but no two pictures are the same color? All of the screens are receiving exactly the same signal but each screen has its own unique way of displaying color (its own unique 'color characteristics'). Different settings on each TV for brightness, contrast and color only make the problem worse.

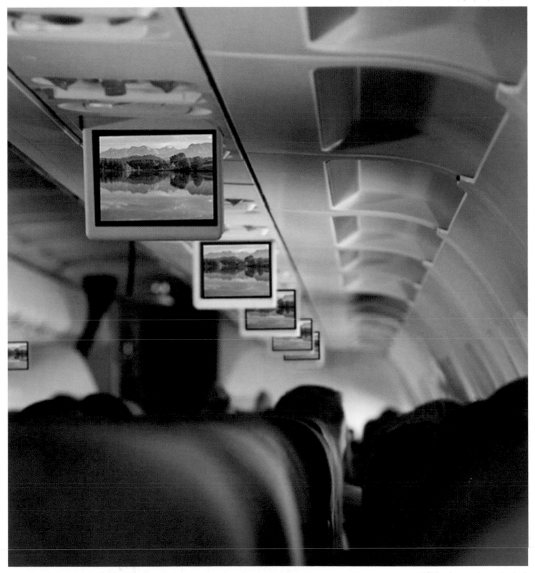

One image displayed with variations of color - the results of a non-color-managed workflow

In photography software and hardware manufacturers such as Adobe have made this elusive world of color consistency possible across all devices by implementing the concept, and workflow, called 'Color Management'. By defining or 'profiling' the color characteristics of each device we can ensure that the same image appears the same on each and every device.

Color management

Color management is the term given to the process of maintaining colors' accuracy from capture to output. The secret to color managed success is to adopt a professional workflow that takes the frustration out of seeing your colors shift as your image moves from camera to monitor, and from monitor to print. Color consistency has never been more easy and affordable to implement and relies on device profiles and the use of color spaces which are device independent.

ProPhoto (white) and Monitor Display (color)

The concept of using a Color Working Space

Color spaces come in all shapes and sizes, from the small (sRGB) to the very large (ProPhoto). A typical digital camera is capable of capturing a range of colors much larger than can be displayed by a typical monitor or output to a typical printer. A working color space can be chosen in the image-editing software that encompasses all of these colors until the user decides where the image is destined to be output. Colors captured by a camera or scanner are converted from the device space into the working space and can then be optimized for a broad range of different output devices. A copy of the image can then be converted to the smaller ouptut color space, as with CMYK conversions, or converted to the output space as the image is being sent to the printer driver.

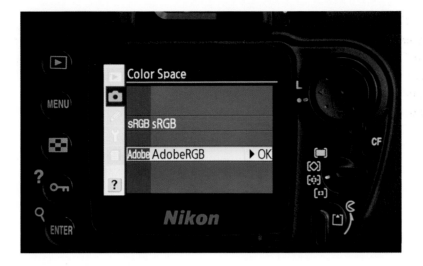

Choosing a color space for the capture device

Select one of two profiles in camera when using the JPEG or TIFF file formats so that the image editing software can know the precise color values that were recorded by the digital camera. The two profiles are Adobe RGB and sRGB. sRGB is the smaller of the two spaces and should only be selected when the user requires images for screen display or automated printing workflows that may be optimized to this profile (popular with consumer quality cameras and the labs that may print these type of images). When capturing in the Raw format these profiles are not embedded in the images. The profiles for the camera reside with the raw editing software and can be applied as part of the post-production editing workflow.

Choosing a Working Space for the image-editing software

In the Color Settings of your editing software you need to choose the working space that best suits your workflow. This can be one of the following three choices:

- Adobe RGB for print.
- sRGB for screen.
- ProPhoto for fine print.

Calibrating and profiling a computer monitor

Every commercial photographer must calibrate and profile their monitor if color accuracy is important to their photographic workflow. The Industry standards are:

Whitepoint (color temperature) - D65
Gamma (mid-tone brightness) - 2.2
Luminance (overall brightness) - 100 to 140 cd/m^2

Note > A standard unit of measurement for luminance is often stated as candela per square metre or cd/m^2.

Straight out of the box just about all monitors are too bright and too blue for photo editing (gray tones are not neutral), so we need to change them to settings that are commonly recognized as 'standard' amongst professional photographers. This process is called 'monitor calibration'. The next part of the process is to measure the color characteristics of your unique monitor so that your image editing software understands how color is displayed on your screen. The color characteristics are saved in a file called a 'color profile' that uses the file extension '.icc'.

Image-editing software such as Adobe Photoshop can then read the monitor profile to ensure that images are displayed accurately on your screen. If the photographer only takes one action to improve their color management it would be to plant the cornerstone of color management - calibrate and profile the monitor you are working on.

Image-editing software such as Photoshop will now display what your camera saw when you first captured the image. Any adjustments you now make to the color or tone of the image will be appropriate and not misguided due to a monitor that has not been calibrated and skews the colors so that they appear incorrect.

White balance

Are the image colors displayed on your computer screen accurate just because the image file and the monitor both have profiles and your image-editing software is managing the colors? Not necessarily. Both of the images above were assigned a profile in the camera but were then assigned different white balance presets (shade on the left and daylight on the right). Auto white balance in the camera makes a guess at the color temperature from the range of colors it is presented with, in each and every frame (variation is the name of the game here). The colors in an image can only really be accurate if the photographer creates a manual white balance from a known value (a neutral tone) or creates a reference image of the color temperature of the light source.

The Expodisc is placed in front of the camera lens and can measure the appropriate exposure and the color temperature of the dominant light source

White balance reference cards such as the WhiBal or products such as the Expodisc can help the professional photographer establish an accurate white balance setting in camera.

Changing the white balance in Adobe Camera Raw

The first step in optimizing the color and tonal values for the color space we have chosen to work in is to set the white balance by choosing one of the presets from the drop-down menu. If a white balance was performed in the camera, the 'As Shot' option can be selected. If none of the presets adjust the color to your satisfaction you can manually adjust the 'Temperature' and 'Tint' sliders to remove any color cast present in the image. The 'Temperature' slider controls the blue/yellow color balance while the 'Tint' slider controls the green/magenta balance. Moving both the sliders in the same direction controls the red/cyan balance.

Alternatively you can simply click on the 'White Balance' eyedropper in the small tools palette (top left-hand corner of the dialog box) and then click on any neutral tone you can find in the image.

Note > Although it is a 'White Balance' you actually need to click on a tone that is not too bright. Clicking on a light or mid gray is preferable.

A photographer looking to save time may introduce a 'gray card' in the first frame of a shoot to simplify the task. If precise white balance is extremely critical the photographer can shoot a Gretag Macbeth ColorChecker Chart that uses a range of color and gray patches. The user can then target the Red, Green and Blue patches and fine-tune the white balance using the Calibrate controls in ACR. Precise measurements for the colors can be found on the website www.brucelindbloom.com

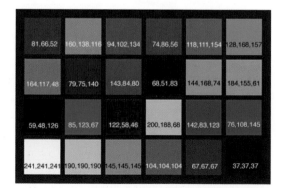

A Gretag Macbeth ColorChecker Chart

Color space

There are four choices of color space in the ACR dialog box and it is important to select the most appropriate one for your workflow before you start to assign color values to the image in ACR (using the controls on the right side of the dialog box). ColorMatch RGB is rarely used these days (it was a space commonly used before color management came of age back at the end of the last decade) so the choice is now limited to just three. The main difference between the three major spaces is the size of the color gamut (the range of colors that each space supports). There is not much point in working with a color space larger than necessary as the colors outside of the monitor space will not be visible and they cannot be reproduced by an output device with a limited gamut range. The three color spaces are as follows:

sRGB – This is the smallest (with a range of colors similar to a typical monitor) of the three common color spaces and should be selected if your images are destined for screen viewing or are destined to be printed by a print service provider using the sRGB color space.

Adobe RGB (1998) – This space is larger than the sRGB space and is the most common color space used in the commercial industry, where the final image is to appear in print. It is a good compromise between the gamut of a color monitor and the gamut of an average CMYK printing press. It is also a space that is suitable for some Print Service Providers and standard quality inkjet prints, e.g. a budget inkjet printer using matte or semi-gloss paper.

The wide gamut ProPhoto space (white) compared to the Adobe RGB (1998) space (color)

ProPhoto RGB – This is the largest color space and can be selected if you have access to a print output device with a broad color gamut (larger than most CMYK devices are capable of offering). When working in ProPhoto the user must stay in 16 Bits/Channel for the entire editing process. Converting to smaller color spaces in Photoshop's main editing space usually results in loss of data in the channels regardless of the rendering intent selected in the conversion process. This loss of data may not be immediately obvious if you do not check the histogram after the conversion process. The data loss is most apparent in bright saturated colors where texture and fine detail may be missing as the color information in the individual channels has become clipped in the conversion process.

Assigning a profile in Adobe Camera Raw

In the full version of Photoshop you can assign a color space to an image in ACR by choosing one of the options in the Workflow Options dialog box. When the image is opened in the main editing space or saved as a TIFF or JPEG the image is tagged with the working space profile. When using ACR in Photoshop Elements the image is tagged with the color space that has been chosen in the Color Settings (Always Optimize for Computer Screens or Always Optimize for Printing). In Photoshop Lightroom the color space is selected in the Export dialog box or automatically when the images are processed for the web galleries.

Note > The native working space in Photoshop Lightroom is 'Melissa RGB' which has the broad color gamut of ProPhoto RGB and the luminance values of sRGB.

Convert images destined for screen presentation to sRGB

If images have been opened in Photoshop and tagged with the Adobe RGB or ProPhoto RGB profile for printing purposes the photographer needs to convert the profile to sRGB if the photographer then decided to use the images for displaying on the web or via another piece of software that is not color managed, e.g PowerPoint. It is important to convert the images to sRGB otherwise the images will appear less saturated when they appear in software that is not color managed. Images that are already open in Photoshop can be batch converted to sRGB by using the Image Processor dialog box. For users of the full version of Photoshop the Image Processor can also be accessed directly from Bridge (Tools > Photoshop > Image Processor).

Saturation and vibrance

The size of the color space dictates how saturated some of the colors can be raised before clipping occurs. Clipping saturated colors can lead to a loss of fine detail and texture. Saturation clipping is especially noticeable when you have selected the smaller sRGB color space and have captured an image with highly saturated colors. The Vibrance slider that has been introduced with recent versions of ACR and Photoshop Lightroom applies a non-linear increase in saturation (targeting pixels of lower saturation). It is also designed to protect skin tones in order to prevent faces from getting too red. It should create less clipping problems when compared to the Saturation control.

High levels of saturation clipping present in this file were corrected with the help of the Saturation controls in the HSL tab - saturation could then be increased reasonably non-destructively using the Vibrance slider.
Image of Melissa Zappa by Victoria Verdon Roe

In images where some colors readily clip due to their natural vibrance (especially when using a smaller gamut such as sRGB), lowering the global saturation in order to protect the clipping of a single color can result in a lifeless image. In these instances the user can turn to the HSL tab to edit the saturation or hue of colors independently.

Note > Choosing a larger color space such as ProPhoto RGB, where the colors rarely clip, is only a short-term solution. The color gamut must eventually be reduced to fit the gamut of the output device. ACR in the full version of Photoshop is currently the best place to massage these colors into the destination space.

last words / last words:

last words.

last

Andrew Boyle

exposure and light meters

Mark Galer

essential skills

~   Gain a knowledge and understanding of exposure and its relationship to light-
    sensitive media, depth of field and selective focus.

~   Understand the use of hand-held and TTL light meters.

~   Understand the difference between reflected and incident meter readings and
    their relationship to lighting ratios and exposure.

~   Create images demonstrating an understanding of metering techniques.

~   Document the progress and development of these skills.

Introduction

An understanding of exposure is without doubt the most critical part of the photographic process. Automatic exposure systems found in many sophisticated camera systems calculate and set the exposure for the photographer. This may lead some individuals to think there is only one correct exposure, when in reality there may be several. The exposure indicated by an automatic system, no matter how sophisticated, is an average. Creative photographers use indicated meter readings for guidance only. Other photographers may interpret the same reading in different ways to create different images. It is essential the photographer understands how the illuminated subject is translated by exposure into a photographic image.

Exposure

Exposure is the action of subjecting a light-sensitive medium to light. Cameras and lenses control the intensity of light (aperture) and the duration of light (time). The intensity of light is determined by the size of the aperture in the lens and the duration of light is determined by the shutter.

Exposure is controlled by aperture and time - intensity and duration.

Too much light will result in overexposure. Too little light will result in underexposure. It makes no difference whether there is a large or a small amount of light, the same amount of light for an appropriate exposure is still required.

Overexposure　　　　　*Correct exposure*　　　　　*Underexposure*
　　　　　　　　　　　- Line Mollerhaug

A digital camera set to manual mode cannot automatically alter its sensitivity to light. Exposure must be adjusted manually. This is achieved by adjusting either the intensity (**aperture**) or duration of light (**time**) or a higher or lower ISO chosen. Increasing the size of the aperture gives more exposure, decreasing gives less. Decreasing the duration of the shutter speed reduces exposure, increasing gives more.

Measuring light

To calculate correct exposure the intensity or level of light has to be measured. Light is measured by a light meter. Understanding the metering techniques of both hand-held light meters and those found in most cameras using their own metering systems is an important skill. All light meters inform the photographer of the amount of light available to obtain an appropriate exposure. This information can be used to set aperture and shutter speed settings in a variety of combinations. Each combination will give different visual outcomes whilst retaining the same overall exposure. Aperture will determine depth of field, shutter speed will determine motion blur. Working in a creative medium such as photography 'correct exposure' can sometimes be a very subjective opinion. The photographer may want the image to appear dark or light to create a specific mood.

Exposing for highlights - Mark Galer

Appropriate exposure

A light meter reading should only be viewed as a guide to exposure. Digital image sensors are unable to record the broad range of tones visible to the human eye. If the camera frames a subject with highlights and shadows the light-sensitive medium may only be able to capture the highlight tones or the shadow tones, not both. An extremely bright tone and an extremely dark tone cannot both record with detail and texture in the same framed image. Underexposure and overexposure in one image is therefore not only possible but common.

It is often necessary for the photographer to take more than one reading to decide on the most appropriate exposure. If a reading is taken of a highlight area the resulting exposure may underexpose the shadows. If a reading is taken of the shadows the resulting exposure may overexpose the highlights. The photographer must therefore decide whether highlight or shadow detail is the priority, change the lighting or reach a compromise. A clear understanding of exposure is essential if the photographer is to make an informed decision.

Intensity and duration

Intensity

Light intensity is controlled by the aperture in the lens. Actual aperture is the size of the diameter of the iris built in to the camera lens. The aperture is a mechanical copy of the iris existing in the human eye. The human iris opens up in dim light and closes down in bright light to control the amount of light reaching the retina. The aperture of the camera lens must also be opened and closed in different brightness levels to control the amount or intensity of light. The right amount of light is required for correct exposure. Too much light and the light-sensitive medium will be overexposed, not enough light and it will be underexposed.

As the aperture on the lens is opened or closed a series of clicks can be felt. These clicks are called f-stops and are numbered. When the value of the f-stop **decreases** by one stop exactly **twice** as much light reaches the image plane as the previous number. When the value of the f-stop **increases** by one stop **half** as much light reaches the image plane as the previous number. The only confusing part is that maximum aperture is the f-stop with the smallest value and minimum aperture is the f-stop with the largest value. The larger the f-stop the smaller the aperture. Easy!

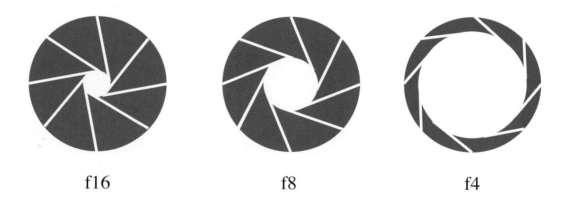

f16   f8   f4

Activity 1

Carefully remove the lens from either a small-format or medium-format camera.
Hold the lens in front of a diffuse light source of low intensity.
Whilst looking through the lens notice how the size of the aperture changes as you alter the f-stop.
Record and discuss the relationship between the size of the aperture and the corresponding f-stop number displayed on the barrel of the lens or in the LCD panel.

Relationship between aperture and f-number

The reasoning behind the values given to the f-stops can be explained by the following example:

- The diameter of a selected aperture on a standard 50mm lens for a 35mm camera measures 12.5mm.
- This measurement divides into the focal length of the lens (50mm) exactly four times.
- The aperture is therefore given the number f4.
- The diameter of another selected aperture on the same lens measures 6.25mm.
- This measurement can similarly be divided into the focal length of the lens to give an f-number of f8 thereby explaining why the higher f-numbers refer to the smaller apertures.

Itti Karuson

The diameter of the same f-number may vary for different focal-length lenses but the intensity of light reaching the image plane remains constant. F4 on a long focal-length lens is physically much larger than the same aperture on a shorter focal-length lens. The intensity of the light reaching the image plane is the same, however, due to the increased distance the light has to travel through the longer focal-length lens. See 'Inverse square law'.

Activity 2

Take exposure readings of a subject in bright sunlight and in deep shade. Record all of the different combinations of exposure for each lighting condition. Compare the results between a fixed focal-length-lens and a zoom lens.

Duration

Light duration is controlled by the shutter. The time the light-sensitive surface is exposed to light is measured in whole and fractions of a second. This time is regulated by the shutter speed. Until the invention of the focal plane shutter, exposure time had been controlled by devices either attached to or within the lens itself. These shutters regulated the length of exposure. Early cameras had no shutter at all and relied upon the photographer removing and replacing a lens cap to facilitate correct exposure times. Other rudimentary shutters, very similar in appearance to miniature roller blinds, were tried but it was not until the invention of a reliable mechanical shutter that exposure times could be relied upon. As film emulsions became faster (increased sensitivity to light) so did the opportunity to make shorter exposures. Within a relatively brief period exposures were no longer in minutes but in fractions of a second.

Mark Galer

The shutter

The main types of shutter systems used in photography are the digital shutter, the leaf shutter and the focal plane shutter. The primary function of all systems is exposure. When the shutter is released it opens for the amount of time set on the shutter speed dial or LCD. These figures are in whole and fractions of seconds. The length of time the shutter is open controls the amount of light reaching the image plane. Each shutter speed doubles or halves the amount of light entering the camera.

Leaving the shutter open for a greater length of time will result in a slower shutter speed. Shutter speeds slower than 1/60 second, using a standard lens, can cause motion blur or camera shake unless you brace the camera or mount it on a tripod.

Using a shutter speed faster than 1/250 or 1/500 second usually requires a wide aperture, more light or image sensor of increased sensitivity. These measures are necessary to compensate for the reduced amount of light passing through a shutter open for a short period of time.

> **The same exposure or level of illumination can be achieved using different combinations of aperture and shutter speed. For example, an exposure of f11 @ 1/125 second = f8 @ 1/250 second = f16 @ 1/60 second, etc.**

Digital shutter

The duration of the exposure can be controlled entirely by electronic means by switching on and switching off the image sensor for the prescribed amount of time. Many digital SLR cameras, however, use a hybrid system of digital and focal plane shutters.

Leaf shutter

Leaf shutters are situated in the lens assembly of most medium-format and all large-format cameras. They are constructed from a series of overlapping metal blades or leaves. When the shutter is released the blades swing fully open for the designated period of time.

Focal plane shutter

A focal plane shutter is situated in the camera body directly in front of the image plane (where the image is focused), hence the name. This system is used extensively in 35mm SLR cameras and a few medium-format cameras. The system can be likened to two curtains, one opening and one closing the shutter's aperture or window. When the faster shutter speeds are used the second curtain starts to close before the first has finished opening. A narrow slit is moved over the image plane at the fastest shutter speed. This precludes the use of high speed flash. If flash is used with the fast shutter speeds only part of the frame is exposed.

The advantages of a focal plane shutter over a leaf shutter are:

- fast shutter speeds in excess of 1/1000 second.
- lenses are comparatively cheaper because they do not require shutter systems.

The disadvantage is:

- limited flash synchronization speeds.

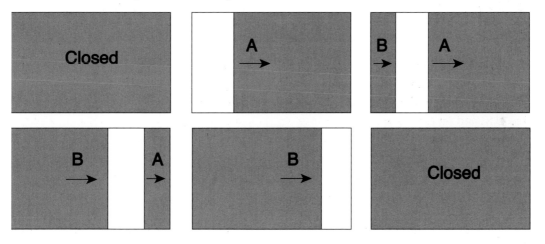

Focal plane shutter firing faster than the fastest flash synchronization speed

Activity 3

Create exposures of a stationary subject at a variety of shutter speeds between 1/125 and 1/4 second whilst hand holding a camera. Use a standard focal-length lens and correct the exposure using the aperture each time the shutter speed is adjusted.

Compare and discuss your results to see who has the least image blur.

Take exposure readings of a subject in bright sunlight and covered shade.

Record all of the different combinations of exposure for each lighting condition.

Hand-held light meters

Accurate exposure is critical to the final quality of the photographic image. It is therefore essential to have a reliable light meter. The ability of the human eye to compensate for variations in light, shade and contrast is far greater than any light-sensitive surface currently available. It is difficult to appreciate how the difference between dark and light tones and the balance between different light sources (lighting ratio) will translate into a photographic image without the use of a meter. Next to a camera the light meter is often considered the most important piece of photographic equipment. Most cameras have built-in metering systems measuring light reflected from the subject. Although very useful, reflected light meters do not provide information to the photographer about the levels of light falling on the subject. Photographers requiring this information need a separate hand-held meter that will measure reflected and incident light. Without a meter only experience will tell you if there will be detail in the shadows or highlights on the final image.

Meter readings

Measuring light for the purpose of exposure can be achieved by taking a reflected or an incident reading.

A **reflected reading** is when the light-sensitive cell of the meter is pointed at the subject and the light reflected from the subject is measured.

An **incident reading** is when the meter's light-sensitive cell is pointed at the camera from the subject and the light falling on the subject is measured. A white plastic diffuser called an '**invercone**' is placed over the meter's light-sensitive cell. The invercone collects the light from a wide angle of view (180°) and transmits 18% of that light to the meter's cell.

Meter-indicated exposure

The indicated exposure reading is known as the '**meter-indicated exposure**' (**MIE**). Although the photographer sees a subject, the meter sees only a level of light. The meter is calibrated to render everything as a mid-tone regardless of the level of illumination. A meter will therefore give 'correct' exposure for a man in a gray flannel suit whether he is in a cellar or sunlight.

18% gray card

The mid-tone to which all meters are calibrated is called an '**18% gray card**', so called because it reflects 18% of the light falling upon it. It is an exposure and color standard manufactured by Kodak. If a meter reading is taken from any single tone the resulting MIE will render the tone as a mid-tone. If a reflected meter reading is taken from a black card the resulting MIE will render the black card gray. If a reflected meter reading is taken from a white card the resulting MIE will render the white card gray. This is why snow often comes out gray in many snapshots.

Taking a hand-held meter reading

Incident reading

For an incident reading it is important to place the white plastic dome supplied with the meter over the light-sensitive cell. This is called an '**invercone**'. The purpose of the invercone is to diffuse the light falling on the subject from a wide angle of acceptance (180°) and transmit 18% of that light. The sensitivity or ISO of the digital image sensor must then be calibrated into the meter. The light meter is generally taken to the subject and the light-sensitive cell is directed back towards the camera. The reading may default to EV (exposure value) which can be interpreted or changed to an aperture/shutter speed combination. On modern digital meters the photographer is able to pre-select a particular shutter speed or aperture and have the meter indicate the corresponding value to obtain correct exposure.

Copyright D. Maynard

Creating an incident reading using the camera's TTL meter

You can place a diffuser such as the 'expodisc' over a camera lens in order to create an incident light meter reading using the camera's own TTL meter. This type of product is also excellent at creating a custom white balance setting or can be used to capture a reference image that can be used to create a white balance setting in Adobe Camera Raw.

Activity 4

Take an incident light reading of a subject in a constant light source.

Note the f-stop at an exposure time of 1/8 second. Increase the number of the aperture by three f-stops.

Note the change in exposure time.

What would the result be if the duration of time had been increased by a factor of three instead of the aperture?

Reflected reading

For a reflected reading it is important to remove the invercone. The meter's cell has an angle of acceptance equal to a standard lens (with a spot meter attachment the angle can be reduced to five degrees or less for precise measurements). The ISO setting is calibrated into the meter. The meter is pointed **towards** the subject. The exposure the meter recommends is an average of the reflected light from the light and dark tones present. When light and dark tones are of equal distribution within the field of view this average reading is suitable for exposure. It must be remembered the meter measures only the level of light. It does not distinguish between dark or light tones. If a reading is taken from a single tone the light meter will always indicate an exposure suitable to render this tone as a mid-tone. If the subject is wearing a gray flannel suit a reflected reading from the camera would give an average for correct exposure. However, if the subject is wearing a white shirt and black jeans a reflected reading of the shirt would give an exposure that would make the shirt appear gray and a reflected reading of the jeans would also make them appear gray. When light or dark tones dominate the photographer must increase or decrease exposure accordingly.

General reflected reading

If the reading is taken from the camera position a general reading results. This general reading is an average between the reflected light from the light and dark tones present. When light and dark tones are of equal distribution within the frame this average light reading is suitable for exposing the subject. When light or dark tones predominate in the image area they overly influence the meter reading and the photographer must increase or decrease exposure accordingly.

Specific reflected reading

A more accurate reading can be taken when light or dark tones dominate the scene by moving the light meter closer to a mid-tone. This avoids the meter being overly influenced by the shadow and highlight tones. Care must be taken not to cast your own shadow or that of the meter when taking a reading from a close surface.

If the photographer is unable to approach the subject being photographed, it is possible to take a meter reading from a tone close to the camera. A useful technique is to take a reading from a gray card angled to reflect the same light as the subject or of Caucasian skin (approximately one stop brighter than a mid-tone).

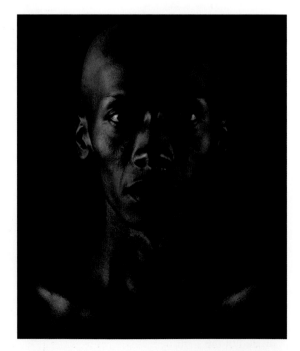

Charanjeet Wadhawa

Understanding the meter reading

There are many ways of understanding the information a light meter is giving in relation to exposure. The meter read-out system itself can be confusing. Some photographers refer to EV (exposure value) readings, others t-stops (transmission) and others in zones. In reality they all mean the same. Of all the variations the most common usage is f-stops. All meters usually default to f-stops and all camera lens apertures are calibrated in f-stops. It is important to understand if the exposure is increased by one stop, either by time or aperture, the amount of light entering the camera has doubled (2x). If increased by two stops the amount of light has doubled again (4x). If increased by three stops the light doubles again (8x) and so on. This simple law applies with the opposite result to decrease in exposure. It is also important to set the meter to the chosen ISO rating (measure of sensitivity to light).

Average exposure

If the lighting is even most image sensors are able to record a full range of tones. Where the tones are evenly distributed the most appropriate exposure is often the average indicated by the light meter. When light or dark tones dominate, however, underexposure or overexposure may occur as the average exposure is no longer appropriate. It is essential to understand how the light meter reads light to have full control over exposure.

Itti Karuson

Activity 5

Using a diffuse light source (cloudy sky) take individual reflected light meter readings of three pieces of card, one white, one black and one mid-gray. Adjust the card to avoid specular reflections (the card should not appear shiny). The black card should give a reading different by four stops to the reading off the white card. The mid-gray card should be between the two. If the mid-gray card is two stops apart from each, you have a mid-tone the meter sees as the average tone (18% gray).
Make an exposure of each of the three cards using the reflected MIE of each card.
Photograph the white and black cards again using the MIE of the gray card.
Label the results with the MIE, the actual exposure and the tone of the card.

TTL light meters

TTL or 'Through-the-lens' light meters, built into cameras, measure the level of reflected light prior to exposure. They measure only the reflected light from the subject matter within the framed image. The meter averages or mixes the differing amounts of reflected light within the framed image, and indicates an average level of reflected light. The light meter readings are translated by the camera's CPU and used to set aperture and/or shutter speed.

Centre-weighted and matrix metering

Centre-weighted and selective metering systems (matrix metering), common in many cameras, bias the information collected from the framed area in a variety of ways. Centre-weighted metering takes a greater percentage of the information from the central area of the viewfinder. The reading, no matter how sophisticated, is still an average - indicating one exposure value only. Any single tone recorded by the photographer using a TTL reading will reproduce as a mid-tone, no matter how dark or light the tone or level of illumination. This tone is the midpoint between black and white. If the photographer takes a photograph of a black or white wall and uses the indicated meter reading to set the exposure, the final image produced would show the wall as having a mid-tone (the same tone as a photographer's 18% gray card).

Centre-weighted TTL metering

Automatic TTL exposure modes

If the camera is set to fully automatic or program mode both the shutter speed and aperture will be set automatically, ensuring an average exposure in response to the level of light recorded by the meter. In low light the photographer using the program mode should be aware of the shutter speed being used to achieve this exposure. As the lens aperture reaches its widest setting the program mode will start to use shutter speeds slower than those usually recommended to avoid camera shake. Many cameras alert the photographer to this using an audible or visual signal. This should not be treated as a signal to stop taking photographs but to take precautions to avoid camera shake, such as bracing the camera or by using a tripod.

Semi-automatic

The disadvantage of a fully automatic or programme mode is it can often take away the creative input the photographer can make to many of the shots. A camera set to fully automatic is programmed to make decisions not necessarily correct for every situation.

If your camera is selecting both the aperture and shutter speed you will need to spend some time finding out how the camera can be switched to semi-automatic and manual operation. Semi-automatic exposure control, whether aperture priority (Av) or shutter priority (Tv), allows creative input from the photographer (**depth of field** and **movement blur**) but still ensures MIE is obtained automatically.

Aperture priority (Av)

This is a semi-automatic function where the photographer chooses the aperture and the camera selects the shutter speed to achieve MIE. This is the most common semi-automatic function used by professional photographers as the depth of field is usually the primary consideration. The photographer using aperture priority needs to be aware of slow shutter speeds being selected by the automatic function of the camera when selecting small apertures in low-light conditions. To avoid camera shake and unintended blur the aperture has to be opened and the depth of field sacrificed.

Kata Bayer

Shutter priority (Tv)

This is a semi-automatic function where the photographer chooses the shutter speed and the camera selects the aperture to achieve correct exposure. In choosing a fast shutter speed the photographer needs to be aware of underexposure as light levels decrease. The fastest shutter speed possible is often limited by the maximum aperture of the lens. In choosing a slow shutter speed the photographer needs to be aware of overexposure when photographing a brightly lit subject. Movement blur may not be possible when using a high ISO in bright conditions.

Interpreting the meter reading

The information given by the light meter after taking a reading is referred to as the '**meter-indicated exposure**' **(MIE).** This is a guide to exposure only. The light meter should not be perceived as having any intelligence or creative sensibilities. The light meter cannot distinguish between tones or subjects of interest or disinterest to the photographer. It is up to the photographer to decide on the most appropriate exposure to achieve the result required. A photographer with a different idea and outcome may choose to vary the exposure. It is the photographer's ability to interpret and vary the meter-indicated exposure to suit the mood and communication of the image that separates their creative abilities from others.

If light or dark tones dominate, the indicated exposure will be greatly influenced by these dominant tones. Using the MIE will expose these dominant dark or light tones as mid-tones. Minority light and mid-tones will be overexposed or underexposed. If you consider interest and visual impact within a photograph is created by the use of lighting and subject contrast (amongst many other things) the chances of all the elements within the frame being mid-tones are remote. The information, mood and communication of the final image can be altered through adjusting exposure from MIE.

Indian market (average tones) MIE

Average tones

A subject of average reflectance (mid-tone) is placed with equal dark and light tones. All three tones are lit equally by the same diffuse light source.

A reflected reading of the mid-tones will give correct exposure. An exposure using the reflected reading of the dark tone will render it gray and overexpose the mid and light tones. An exposure using the reflected reading of the light tone will render it gray and underexpose the mid and dark tones.

An incident reading will give 'correct' exposure regardless of which tone it is held in front of because it measures the light falling on the subject, not the light reflected from it. The intensity of the light source is constant but the reflected light from the three tones varies (see page 40, Hand-held light meters).

Dominant tones

If dark tones dominate the framed image the MIE will result in the dark tones being recorded as mid-tones. Mid-tones will be recorded as light tones and any light tones may be overexposed. If light tones dominate the framed image the meter-indicated exposure will result in the light tones being recorded as mid-tones. Mid-tones will be recorded as dark tones and dark tones may be underexposed. If the mid-tones present in amongst these dominant dark or light tones are to be recorded accurately the exposure must be either reduced (for dominant dark tones) or increased (for dominant light tones) from the MIE.

Black swan (dominant dark tones) MIE

Decreased exposure

White wall (dominant light tones) MIE

Increased exposure

The amount the exposure needs to be reduced or increased is dictated by the level of dominance of these dark or light tones (see the chapter 'Contrast and Compensation > Exposure compensation').

Activity 6

Photograph a subject requiring adjusted exposure from that indicated by the light meter. State how the dominant tones would have affected the light meter reading and how the image would have looked if you had not adjusted the exposure.

Reading exposure levels

When taking a picture with a digital camera it is sometimes possible to check the exposure during the capture stage to ensure that the full tonal range of the image has been recorded. The most accurate indication of the exposure does not come from the image on the LCD screen but the histogram (all DSLR cameras and the better fixed-lens compact cameras are able to display these histograms). Some fixed-lens cameras can even display the histogram before the image has been captured. This 'live preview' is also available on a few DSLR cameras that have a second sensor designed to feed this live view to the LCD screen prior to capture.

The levels of brightness in the histogram are displayed as a simple graph. The horizontal axis displays the brightness values from left (darkest) to right (lightest). The vertical axis of the graph shows how much of the image is found at any particular brightness level. If the subject contrast is too high or the exposure is either too high or too low then tonality will be 'clipped' (shadow or highlight detail will be lost). Most digital camera sensors can only record a limited range of information when compared to the range of tones human vision is capable of seeing detail in. The tones that are out of the range of the image sensor of the digital camera record as black or white with no detail. We should attempt to adjust the exposure or reduce the contrast of the subject matter to ensure maximum information is recorded.

Note > When using the JPEG file format you should attempt to modify the brightness, contrast and color balance at the capture stage to obtain the best possible histogram before editing begins in the software.

Correcting exposure

The photographer can either increase or decrease exposure to ensure a full range of tones is recorded during the capture stage. Photoshop will not be able to replace information in the shadows or highlights that is missing due to inappropriate exposure or excessive subject contrast. The information should extend all the way from the left to the right side of the histogram if the subject contrast and the exposure are appropriate.

Overexposure and underexposure

If the exposure is too high a tall peak will be seen to rise on the right side of the histogram (level 255). If the digital file is underexposed the peaks are crowded on the left-hand side of the histogram and there is little or no peaks on the right-hand side of the histogram. Some cameras can be programed to blink in the areas that are overexposed.

Solution: Adjust the exposure in the camera using either the exposure compensation controls or the manual controls. If exposure is too low due to bright backlights in the image you can try moving the camera to exclude the bright light source, locking the exposure by half-pressing the shutter release and then reframing.

Lowering contrast

If the contrast is too high tall peaks may be evident at either end of the histogram.

Solution: Decrease the subject contrast by either repositioning the subject matter or by lowering the contrast of the lighting. The light source can be diffused or additional lighting can be provided in the form of fill flash or reflectors. In the image above the camera's tiny built-in flash unit has been used to increase the exposure in the shadows. This allows the overall exposure to be lowered, which in turn prevents the sky behind the children from becoming overexposed.

Optimizing a histogram after capture

The final histogram should show that pixels have been allocated to most, if not all, of the 256 levels. If the histogram indicates large gaps between the ends of the histogram and the sliders (indicating either a low-contrast scan or low-contrast subject photographed in flat lighting) the relationship between the subject contrast and light quality could be reconsidered.

Small gaps at either end of the histogram can, however, be corrected by dragging the sliders to the start of the tonal information. Holding down the Alt/Option key when dragging these sliders will indicate what, if any, information is being clipped. Note how the sliders have been moved beyond the short thin horizontal line at either end of the histogram. These low levels of pixel data are often not representative of the broader areas of shadows and highlights within the image and can usually be clipped (moved to 0 or 255).

Moving the 'Gamma' slider can modify the brightness of the mid-tones. If you select a Red, Green or Blue channel (from the Channel pull-down menu) prior to moving the Gamma slider you can remove a color cast present in the image. For those unfamiliar with color correction the adjustment feature 'Variations' (Image > Adjustments > Variations) in Photoshop gives a quick and easy solution to the problem. After correcting the tonal range using the sliders click 'OK' in the top right-hand corner of the Levels dialog box.

Note > Variations is not available for Photoshop users working in 16 Bits/Channel mode.

Color

Neutral tones in the image should appear desaturated on the monitor. If a color cast is present try to remove it at the time of capture or scanning if possible.

Solution: Control color casts by using either the white balance on the camera (digital) or by using an 80A or 80B color conversion filter when using tungsten light with daylight film. Use the available color controls on the scanning device to correct the color cast and/or saturation.

Raw format exposure considerations

One of the big topics of conversation since the release of Photoshop CS has been the subject of 'Raw' files and 'digital negatives'. This section of the chapter guides you through the advantages of choosing the Raw format and the steps you need to take to process a Raw file from your camera in order to optimize its exposure.

All digital cameras capture in Raw but only digital SLRs and the medium- to high-end 'Prosumer' cameras offer the user the option of saving the images in this Raw format. Selecting the Raw format in the camera instead of JPEG or TIFF stops the camera from processing the color data collected from the sensor. Digital cameras typically process the data collected by the sensor by applying the white balance, sharpening and contrast settings set by the user in the camera's menus. The camera then compresses the bit depth of the color data from 12 to 8 bits per channel before saving the file as a JPEG or TIFF file. Selecting the Raw format prevents this image processing taking place. The Raw data is what the sensor 'saw' before the camera processes the image, and many photographers have started to refer to this file as the 'digital negative'. The term 'digital negative' is also used by Adobe for their archival format (.dng) for Raw files.

Camera Raw

The sceptical among us would now start to juggle with the concept of paying for a 'state-of-the-art' camera to collect and process the data from the image sensor, only to stop the high-tech image processor from completing its 'raison d'être'. If you have to process the data some time to create a digital image why not do it in the camera? The idea of delaying certain decisions until they can be handled in the image-editing software is appealing to many photographers, but the real reason for choosing to shoot in Camera Raw is QUALITY.

Processing Raw data

The unprocessed Raw data can be converted into a usable image file format by Adobe Camera Raw (ACR). Variables such as bit depth, white balance, exposure, brightness, contrast, saturation, sharpness, noise reduction and even the crop can all be assigned as part of the conversion process. Performing these image-editing tasks on the full high-bit Raw data (rather than making these changes after the file has been processed by the camera) enables the user to achieve a higher quality end-result.

Double-clicking a Raw file, or selecting 'Open in Camera Raw' in Bridge, opens the Adobe Camera Raw (ACR) dialog box, where the user can prepare and optimize the file for final processing in the main Photoshop editing interface. If the user selects 16 Bits/Channel in the Workflow Options, the 12 bits per channel data from the image sensor is rounded up - each channel is now capable of supporting 32,769 levels* instead of the 256 levels we are used to working with in the 8 bits per channel option. Choosing the 16 Bits/Channel option enables even more manipulation in the main Photoshop editing space without the risk of degrading the image quality. When the file is opened into the image-editing work-space of your Photoshop software, the Raw file closes. Any changes you make to the appearance of the image in the ACR dialog box will be applied to the image that is opened in Photoshop's main editing space but won't alter the original image data of the Raw file. The adjustments you make in the ACR dialog box are saved as XMP metadata in the DNG file as an XMP sidecar file or in the computer's Camera Raw database or cache.

*Note > Photoshop's 16-bit editing is 15-bit + 1 (15-bit processing gave the Photoshop engineers a midpoint). In Photoshop CS2 we had the option to set the Info palette to 16-bit values to confirm this but this option was removed for Photoshop CS3.

Distribution of data

Most digital imaging sensors capture images using 12 bits of memory dedicated to each of the three RGB color channels, resulting in 4096 tones between black and white. Most of the imaging sensors in digital cameras record a subject brightness range of approximately five to eight stops (five to eight f-stops between the brightest highlights with detail and the deepest shadow tones with detail).

Tonal distribution in 12-bit capture

Darkest Shadows	- 4 stops	- 3 stops	- 2 stops	-1 stop	Brightest Highlights

⟵——— 25% of all levels ————————⟶ ⟵——— 75% of all levels ———⟶

Distribution of levels

One would think that with all of this extra data the problem of banding or image posterization due to insufficient levels of data (a common problem with 8-bit image editing) would be consigned to history. Although this is the case with mid-tones and highlights, shadows can still be subject to this problem. The reason for this is that the distribution of levels assigned to recording the range of tones in the image is far from equitable. The brightest tones of the image (the highlights) use the lion's share of the 4096 levels available while the shadows are comparatively starved of information.

An example of posterization or banding

Shadow management

CCD and CMOS chips are, however, linear devices. This linear process means that when the amount of light is halved, the electrical stimulation to each photoreceptor on the sensor is also halved. Each f-stop reduction in light intensity halves the amount of light that falls onto the receptors compared to the previous f-stop. Fewer levels are allocated by this linear process to recording the darker tones. Shadows are 'level starved' in comparison to the highlights that have a wealth of information dedicated to the brighter end of the tonal spectrum. So rather than an equal amount of tonal values distributed evenly across the dynamic range, we actually have the effect as shown above. The deepest shadows rendered within the scene often have fewer than 128 allocated levels, and when these tones are manipulated in post-production Photoshop editing there is still the possibility of banding or posterization.

Accessing a broader dynamic range

The histogram displayed on the back of a digital camera may not accurately reflect the precise range of tones that is being captured when the photographer elects to shoot in the Camera Raw format. Most cameras provide information that is geared to the photographer capturing in the JPEG or TIFF format only. A photographer may therefore underestimate the dynamic range that is capable of being recorded by their camera. Instead of capturing a dynamic range of approximately five stops the Raw format may be capable of capturing images with a dynamic range that exceeds 7 or 8 stops when using a DSLR camera. The precise dynamic range will vary with the type of sensor being used as the smaller sensors fitted to the prosumer digicams do not enjoy the same dynamic range as the APS and full-frame sensors fitted to the DSLR cameras.

In the example above the highlights of the distant clouds were flashing when the image was reviewed in the camera (a common option on many digital cameras for indicating when overexposure has occurred). The histogram associated with the file clearly indicated that the highlights were being clipped. When the file was opened in Camera Raw the Exposure slider was moved to a value of −0.50 and usable detail (level 245) was returned to this area of the image. The Brightness slider was raised to compensate for the negative Exposure value. If the exposure had been lowered in camera the dark top that the boy is wearing would have required rescuing instead of the highlights. Most photographers find that it is preferable to rescue the highlights rather than the shadows although due care must be taken not to allow the highlights to become completely overexposed. Taking two spot meter readings will enable the experienced photographer to ascertain the subject brightness range and assess whether this is compatible with the dynamic range of the sensor they are using.

Lowering exposure in ACR

For those digital photographers interested in the dark side, an old SLR loaded with a fine-grain black and white film is a hard act to follow. The liquid smooth transitions and black velvet-like quality of dark low-key prints of yesteryear are something that digital capture is hard pressed to match. The sad reality of digital capture is that underexposure in low light produces an abundance of noise and banding (steps rather than smooth transitions of tone). The answer, however, is surprisingly simple for those who have access to a DSLR and have selected the Raw format from the Quality menu settings in their camera. Simply be generous with your exposure to the point of clipping or overexposing your highlights and only attempt to lower the exposure of the shadows in Adobe Camera Raw.

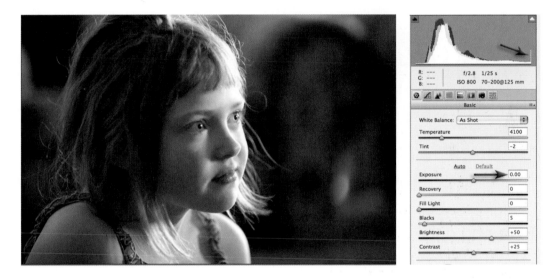

1. The first step is the most difficult to master for those who are used to using Auto or Program camera exposure modes. Although the final outcome may require deep shadow tones, the aim in digital low-key camera exposure is to first get the shadow tones away from the left-hand wall of the histogram by increasing and NOT decreasing the exposure. It is vitally important, however, not to increase the exposure so far that you lose or clip highlight detail. The original exposure of the image used in this project reveals that the shadow tones (visible as the highest peaks in the histogram) have had a generous exposure in-camera so that noise and banding have been avoided (the tones have moved well to the right in the histogram). The highlights, however, look as though they have become clipped or overexposed. The feedback from the histogram on the camera's LCD would have confirmed the clipping at the time of exposure (the tall peak on the extreme right-hand side of the histogram) and if you had your camera set to warn you of overexposure, the highlights would have been merrily flashing at you to ridicule you of your sad attempts to expose this image. The typical DSLR camera is, however, a pessimist when it comes to clipped highlights and ignorant of what is possible in Adobe Camera Raw. Adobe Camera Raw can recover at least one stop of extra highlight information when the Exposure slider is dragged to the left (so long as the photographer has used a DSLR camera that has a broader dynamic range than your typical fixed-lens compact digicam).

Adobe Camera Raw rescues the highlights - sometimes automatically

'Exposing right'

When the Auto checkbox in the Exposure slider is checked, Adobe Camera Raw often attempts to rescue overexposed highlights automatically. With a little knowledge and some attention to the camera's histogram during the capture stage, you can master the art of pushing your highlights to the edge. So if your model is not in a hurry (mine is watching a half-hour TV show) you can take an initial exposure on Auto and then check your camera for overexposure. Increase the exposure using the exposure compensation dial on the camera until you see the flashing highlights. When the flashing highlights start to appear you can still add around one extra stop to the exposure before the highlights can no longer be recovered in Adobe Camera Raw. The popular term for this peculiar behavior is called 'exposing right'.

PERFORMANCE TIP.
If the highlights are merrily flashing and the shadows are still banked up against the left-hand wall of the histogram, the solution is to increase the amount of fill light, i.e. reduce the difference in brightness between the main light source and the fill light (see Lighting on Location > Fill flash).

2. Before we massage the tones to create our low-key image we must first check that our tones are smooth and free from color and luminance noise. Zoom in to 100% magnification for an accurate preview and look for any problems in the smooth dark-toned areas. Setting both the Luminance Smoothing and Color Noise Reduction sliders to 25 (found in the Detail tab) removes the noise in this image. I would also recommend that the Sharpness slider be set to 0 at this point. Rather than committing to global sharpening using the Adobe Camera Raw dialog box, selective sharpening in the main Photoshop editing space may help to keep the tones as smooth as possible.

3. Create the low-key look by moving the Exposure and/or the Brightness sliders to the left in the Basic tab. You can continue to drop these sliders until the highlights start to move away from the right-hand wall of the histogram. Select the 'White Balance Tool' and move your mouse cursor over the deeper shadows - this will give you an idea of the RGB values you are likely to get when this image is opened into the editing space. Once you approach an average of 15 to 20 in all three channels the low-key look should have been achieved.

Expose right and adjust left

'Expose right' and multiple exposures

As we have seen in the previous example the inequitable distribution of levels has given rise to the idea of 'exposing right'. This work practice encourages the user seeking maximum quality to increase the camera exposure of the shadows (without clipping the highlights) so that more levels are afforded to the shadow tones. This approach to making the shadows 'information rich' involves increasing the amount of fill light (actual light rather than the ACR's fill light) or lighting with less contrast in a studio environment. If the Camera Raw file is then opened in the Camera Raw dialog box the shadow values can then be reassigned their darker values to expand the contrast before opening it as a 16 Bits/Channel file. When the resulting shadow tones are edited and printed, the risk of visible banding in the shadow tones is greatly reduced.

Separate exposures can be combined in Adobe Photoshop

This approach is not possible when working with a subject with a fixed subject brightness range, e.g. a landscape, but in these instances there is often the option of bracketing the exposure and merging the highlights of one digital file with the shadows of a second. The example above shows the use of a layer mask to hide the darker shadows in order to access the bit-rich shadows of the underlying layer and regain the full tonal range of the scene. See *Photoshop CS3: Essential Skills* or *Photoshop Elements 6 Maximum Performance* for detailed post-production editing techniques.

Daniel Tückmantel

Paul Allister

contrast and compensation

James Newman

essential skills

~ Gain knowledge and understanding about contrast and exposure compensation and its relationship to the correct exposure.

~ Understand the relationship between lighting contrast, lighting ratios, subject contrast and subject brightness range.

~ Create images demonstrating an understanding of contrast and exposure compensation.

~ Document the progress and development of these skills.

Contrast

The human eye simultaneously registers a wide range of light intensity. Due to their limited latitude image sensors are unable to do this. The difference in the level of light falling on or being reflected by a subject is called contrast. When harsh directional light strikes a subject the overall contrast increases. The highlights continue to reflect high percentages of the increased level of illumination whilst the shadows reflect little extra. Without contrast photographic images can appear dull and flat. It is contrast within the image that gives dimension, shape and form. Awareness and the ability to understand and control contrast is essential to work successfully in the varied and complex situations arising in photography.

- Subject contrast
- Lighting contrast
- Brightness range.

Subject contrast

Different surfaces reflect different amounts of light. A white shirt reflects more light than black jeans. The greater the difference in the amount of light reflected the greater the subject contrast or 'reflectance range'. Reflectance range is best measured when the subject is evenly lit. The difference between the lightest and darkest tones can be measured in stops. If the difference between the white shirt and the black jeans is three stops then eight times more light is being reflected by the shirt than by the jeans (a reflectance range of 8:1).

One stop = 2:1, two stops = 4:1, three stops = 8:1, four stops = 16:1

Paul Allister

Mark Galer

A 'high-contrast' image is where the ratio between the lightest and darkest elements is 32:1 or greater.

A 'low-contrast' image is where the ratio between the lightest and darkest elements is less than 16:1.

Lighting contrast

When harsh directional light strikes a subject the overall contrast increases. The highlights continue to reflect high percentages of the increased level of illumination whilst the shadows reflect little extra.

Overall image contrast therefore is determined by the combined effects of subject contrast or reflectance range and the 'lighting contrast'.

Lighting contrast describes the difference in the level of illumination between the main directional light (key light) and any light falling on the shadows (fill light). The difference can be measured in stops and recorded as a 'lighting ratio'. If the difference between the light illuminating the highlights and the light illuminating the shadows is two stops, the lighting ratio is given as 4:1, i.e. four times more light strikes the tones facing the light as the same tones in the shadows. This is easily measured by taking an incident light meter reading in the light and then in the shadows.

Rodrick Bond

On location - when there is cloud covering the sun the light is diffused or softened. The difference between a tone placed in the diffused light and open shade (away from structures and large objects) may be less than one stop, giving a lighting ratio of less than 2:1. The lighting may be described as being flat and the lighting contrast as low.

When direct sunlight strikes the subject the difference between a tone placed in the sun and the same tone placed in covered shade may increase beyond two stops or 4:1. This directional light creating highlights and shadows is described as high contrast.

In the studio - lighting contrast is controlled by the photographer. The direction, intensity, degree of diffusion and amount of fill light will all be deciding factors in creating a lighting ratio suitable for the desired lighting contrast range.

Stops difference	Light ratio	Stops difference	Light ratio
$\frac{2}{3}$	1.6:1	2	4:1
1	2:1	$2\frac{1}{3}$	5:1
$1\frac{1}{3}$	2.5:1	$2\frac{2}{3}$	6:1
$1\frac{2}{3}$	3:1	3	8:1

Brightness range

Light is reflected unevenly off surfaces, light tones reflecting more light than dark tones. Each subject framed by the photographer will include a range of tones. The broader the range of tones the greater the contrast.

When harsh directional light such as sunlight strikes a subject the overall contrast of the scene increases. The tones facing the light source continue to reflect high percentages of the increased level of illumination whilst the shadows may reflect little extra. The overall contrast of the framed subject is called the SBR or 'subject brightness range'.

SBR of approximately five stops (32:1)   *SBR of approximately three stops (8:1)*

The SBR can be measured by taking a meter reading of the lightest and darkest tones. If the lightest tone reads f16 @ 1/125 second and the darkest tone reads f4 @ 1/125 second the difference is four stops or 16:1.

A subject with a high or extreme brightness range can exceed the latitude of the image sensor

Latitude

Image sensors are capable of recording a limited tonal range or brightness range. A subject photographed in high-contrast lighting may exceed this recordable or 'dynamic range'. The ability for the image sensor to accommodate a brightness range is referred to as its 'latitude'. Digital image sensors capturing JPEG images typically capture a brightness range of only 32:1 or five stops. It is essential for digital photographers to understand that when capturing JPEG images with directional sunlight, shadow and highlight detail may be lost. The photographer capturing Raw files has increased flexibility to capture a broader range of tones, and with careful exposure, post-production processing and printing techniques they can extend this range dramatically.

SBR exceeding the latitude of the image sensor

Previsualization

Awareness of the subject brightness range and the capability of the photographic medium to capture this range of tones allows the photographer to previsualize or predict the outcome of the final image. When the brightness range exceeds the sensor's capabilities the photographer has the option to increase or decrease exposure to protect shadow or highlight detail that would otherwise not record or switch to Raw capture when using a DSLR. These scenes are described as 'extreme contrast'.

Extreme contrast

In an attempt to previsualize the final outcome of a scene with a high brightness range, many photographers use the technique of squinting or narrowing the eyes to view the scene. This technique removes detail from shadows and makes the highlights stand out from the general scene. In this way the photographer is able to predict the contrast of the resulting image. If the photographer fails to take into account the image sensor's limited capabilities both shadow detail and highlight detail can be lost. It is usual for photographers to protect the highlight detail in the exposure and fill the shadow detail with additional lighting .

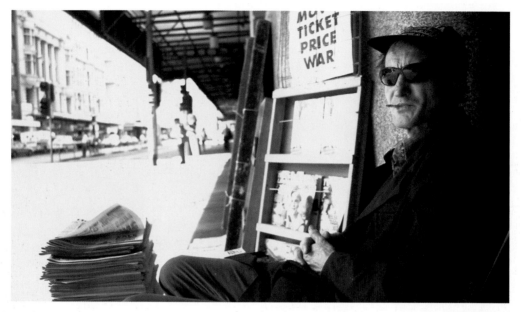

Mark Galer

In many instances when the photographer is expected to work quickly it is all the photographer can do to notice the extreme brightness range and make quick judgements from experience to alter the exposure. The least appropriate exposure in extreme contrast situations is often the exposure indicated by a camera's TTL meter. This average exposure may not be suitable if the subject or detail is located in the deep shadows or bright highlights. In these instances the photographer must override the exposure indicated by the meter and either open up (increase exposure) if shadow detail is required, or stop down (decrease exposure) if highlight detail is required.

In the photograph above the lighting contrast between the noon sun and the shadows was too great to record using the JPEG format. Increased exposure over the indicated meter reading was required to capture the shadow detail.

Activity 1

Create an image where the tonal range of the subject will exceed the tonal range that can be recorded onto the image sensor. Indicate whether the exposure has been increased or decreased from the TTL meter-indicated exposure.

Exposure compensation

When working on location the lighting (sunlight) already exists. There is often little the photographer can do to lower the brightness range. In these instances exposure compensation is often necessary to protect either shadow or highlight detail. The results of exposure compensation are easily assessed via the camera's LCD monitor. The amount of compensation necessary will vary depending on the level of contrast present and what the photographer is trying to achieve. Compensation is usually made in 1/3 or 1/2 stop increments but when a subject is back lit and TTL metering is used the exposure may need increasing by two or more stops depending on the lighting contrast. Remember:

Increasing exposure will reveal more detail in the shadows and dark tones.
Decreasing exposure will reveal more detail in the highlights and bright tones.

Orien Harvey

Exposure compensation adjustment

A compensation setting is required when the photographer wishes to continue working with an automatic metering system instead of manual controls. Using an automatic metering mode the photographer cannot simply adjust the exposure, from that indicated by the meter, using the aperture or shutter speed. The automatic mode will simply re-compensate for the adjustment in an attempt to record the overall tone of the framed subject matter as a mid-tone equal to the 18% gray card.

Assessing the degree of compensation

Photographers calculate the degree of compensation from MIE in a variety of different ways.

Digital histogram - Most DSLR cameras and high-end prosumer digicams allow the user to view a 'histogram' of the exposure immediately after capture and/or indication of highlight clipping (overexposure). In the case of some cameras the histogram can be viewed live with the preview before capture takes place. This is now the most popular method for assessing whether exposure compensation is required when capturing images with digital cameras. It is worth noting, however, that DSLR cameras shooting in the Raw format are capable of capturing a broader dynamic range than the histogram may indicate (see the chapter 'Exposure'). Although this is a reliable method for assessing appropriate exposure compensation it does not replace some of the traditional methods where compensation must be immediate and accurate.

Bracketing - The photographer can estimate the necessary compensation by bracketing the exposures. To bracket the exposure the photographer must expose several frames, varying the exposure in 1/3 or 1/2 stop increments either side of the MIE.

18% Gray card - Photographers can use a mid-tone of known value from which to take a reflected light meter reading. A mid-tone of 18% reflectance is known as a 'gray card'. The gray card must be at the same distance from the light source as the subject. Care must be taken to ensure the shadow of neither the photographer nor the light meter is cast on the gray card when taking the reading. The indicated exposure is suitable for an SBR not exceeding 32:1. If highlight or shadow detail is required the exposure must be adjusted accordingly. When capturing an image in black and white the indicated exposure is suitable for an SBR not exceeding 128:1. If the SBR exceeds 128:1 the exposure can be increased and the subsequent development time decreased. See 'The Zone System'.

Polaroid - Working with some medium-format cameras, a photographer has the added advantage of being able to use Polaroid to assess exposure and composition. Most film has a Polaroid of equal ISO and comparative contrast range. To best understand the relationship between Polaroid and film testing of both is recommended. This will give you the best correlation between how the correct exposure for film would appear on an equivalent Polaroid. Polaroid film holders (backs) fit most medium- and all large-format cameras. Polaroid backs suitable for small-format cameras are limited.

Re-framing - If the photographer is working quickly to record an unfolding event or activity the photographer may have little or no time to bracket or take an average mid-tone reading. In these circumstances the photographer may take a reading quickly from a scene of average reflectance close to the intended subject. This technique of re-framing may also include moving closer to the primary subject matter in order to remove the light source and the dominant light or dark tones from the framed area. Many modern cameras feature an exposure lock to enable the photographer to find a suitable exposure from the environment and lock off the metering system from new information as the camera is repositioned.

Judgement - The fastest technique for exposure compensation is that of judgement, gained from experience and knowledge. The photographer must previsualize the final image and estimate the degree of compensation required to produce the desired effect.

Compensation for back lighting

The most common instance requiring exposure compensation is 'back lighting' using a TTL meter. The metering system will be overly influenced by the light source and indicate a reduced exposure. As the light source occupies more and more of the central portion of the viewfinder so the indicated exposure is further reduced. The required exposure for the subject may be many times greater than the indicated exposure.

Mark Galer

If the camera is in manual mode or equipped with an exposure lock, the photographer can meter for the specific tonal range required and then re-frame the shot. An alternative used by many professionals is to adjust the exposure using the exposure compensation facility. Using this technique can avoid re-framing after first metering.

Activity 2

Choose four different lighting situations where the subject is back lit.

Take a photograph of each subject with the 'meter-indicated exposure' or MIE.

Do not reposition the frame. Make a record of the exposures.

Using your own judgement compensate the exposure using either the exposure compensation facility or adjusting ISO. Make a record of the exposures.

Take a meter reading for the shadow area and with the camera set to manual make one exposure at this reading. Make a record of the exposure.

Take a meter reading for the highlight area and with the camera set to manual make one exposure at this reading. Make a record of the exposure.

Review the images and name the image files accordingly.

Assess the results of your images using exposure compensation.

Recovery and Fill Light in Adobe Camera Raw and Lightroom

The Recovery and Fill Light sliders can rescue bright highlights that have become clipped and dark shadows that may otherwise be too dark to print. When the contrast of the scene is very high (bright sunlight) many good quality digital cameras can be set to warn us of overexposure by blinking the overexposed highlights. Sometimes we can lower the contrast by using a reflector or fill flash and sometimes we can rescue the highlights in Adobe Camera Raw. In the illustration above the highlight warning has been switched on by clicking on the triangle in the top right-hand corner of the histogram window. The red color indicates overexposure (pixels that would be rendered 255 if left unadjusted). Dragging the Recovery slider to the right brings these overexposed tones back under 255 and will allow them to print with texture and detail.

Great care needs to be taken when using the Fill Light slider to rescue dark shadow tones. In this example an extreme adjustment is being made to rescue the shadow tones that have been accidentally underexposed due to the bright tones in the centre of the viewfinder. Be careful with raising the Fill Light value too high, especially with photos taken with a high ISO, as Fill Light will also brighten noise in the photo and make it more apparent. Photos taken at a lower ISO, like ISO 100, will be more forgiving to the Fill Light slider and not expose problems like noise and tonal banding so readily.

Summary of exposure compensation
Hand-held light meters

A hand-held reflected light meter reading measures the level of light reflected from the subject. The resulting exposure is an average between the light and dark tones present. When light and dark tones are of equal distribution this average reading is suitable for exposure. When light or dark tones dominate the photographer must either take a reflected meter reading of a known mid-tone and compensate accordingly, or take an incident reading of the light falling on the subject.

TTL meters

The 'through-the-lens' (TTL) light meter measures the level of reflected light from the subject. The TTL meter does not measure the level of illumination (ambient light). The resulting exposure is an average between the light and dark tones present. When light and dark tones are of equal distribution within the frame this average light reading is suitable for exposing the subject. When light or dark tones dominate the photographer must either meter a known mid-tone or compensate the exposure accordingly.

Summary of exposure compensation

Dominant light tones	increase exposure
Dominant dark tones	decrease exposure

Extreme contrast

Color film/image sensor	
Increase highlight detail	decrease exposure
Increase shadow detail	increase exposure

Black and white negative	
SBR exceeding 128:1	increase exposure and reduce development time

Activity 3

Place a small subject of dominant mid-tones one metre from a bright white background. Light with a diffuse light source (floodlight) and take a reflected light reading from the camera position.
Next take a reflected light reading of the subject only.
Test your judgement by determining correct exposure and exposing one frame only.

Amelia Soegijono

Stuart Wilson

sensitivity and image capture

Martin Ryner

essential skills

~ Gain a knowledge and understanding of the various light-sensitive mediums
   available to the photographer.
~ Understand the use of these materials and devices, their advantages,
   limitations and processing.
~ Create images using technique, observation and selection demonstrating a
   practical understanding of light-sensitive mediums.
~ Document the progress and development of these skills.

Introduction

There is an overwhelming range of image capture mediums now available to the professional and amateur photographer. These range from digital image sensors to various color and black and white film emulsions. Choosing the appropriate medium for the job is an essential skill for every photographer.

Capture mediums

Light-sensitive surfaces can be divided into four main types:

- Digital image sensors
- Black and white negative
- Color negative
- Color transparency (positive or slide film).

Digital image sensors are not interchangeable but most digital cameras allow alteration of the image sensor to its degree of sensitivity to light (ISO setting) and 'white balance' adjustments to allow for different light sources used in the illumination of the subject.

Color negative and color transparency films are distinguished by a number of identifying labels. Films ending with the suffix 'chrome', e.g. Ektachrome, Fujichrome, are transparency films. Film names ending with the suffix 'color' are negative films, e.g. Fujicolor, Kodacolor.

Film boxes will indicate the type of processing required for the film. C-41 indicates the film is a color negative film whilst E-6 indicates the film is a transparency reversal film. Mini-labs are gradually phasing out film processing in favor of digital output, leaving E-6 processing to the professional labs.

35mm and full frame
DSLR image sensor

645

Relative size of formats 67

Each main film type (negative or positive) is available in 35mm, 120 roll film and 4" x 5" sheet film. 120 roll film is suitable for the entire range of medium-format cameras from the smaller 6 x 4.5cm cameras to the popular 6 x 6cm and 6 x 7cm cameras through to the specialist panoramic cameras shooting frames as wide as 6 x 17cm.

Capture formats

Format refers to the size and shape of an image. A certain amount of confusion can surround this term. It applies to both '**camera format**' and '**image format**'. An image can be taken or cropped in the vertical or horizontal format using different format image sensors.

A vertical image (one that is tall and narrow) is described as '**portrait format**' even if the image is a natural landscape. A horizontal image is described as '**landscape format**' even if the subject is a portrait. The origins of this terminology date back to when traditional artists were a little more conservative with their intended use of the frame.

In editorial work photographers must ensure that images are taken using both vertical and horizontal formats. This gives the graphic artists the flexibility to design creative pages.

Most prosumer digicams and some DSLRs currently available (Olympus and Panasonic) use sensors that have a 4:3 format or 'aspect ratio'. The aspect ratio is a numerical way of describing the shape of the frame. A 4:3 aspect ratio means that for every unit of height, the width is one and a third times wider. 4:3 is a numerical description of this ratio without using fractions. This aspect ratio may be also be listed as 1.33:1 (this is another way of defining an aspect ratio, i.e. dividing the width by the height). This format is the same as a standard computer screen, e.g. 1024 x 769 pixels. All of the DSLRs made by Canon, Nikon and Sony have image sensors with a 3:2 aspect ratio that matches 35mm film (although only a few of the sensors, described as full frame, are the same size as 35mm film). This is a slightly wider format than 4:3 but not as wide as a wide-screen television that has a 16:9 aspect ratio. Some prosumer digicams now offer 3:2 as an alternative aspect ratio (usually cropped from the 4:3 format in camera) whilst some digicams use a CCD image sensor with a 16:9 format. The aspect ratio of a single page in this book is close to 4:3 whilst a double-page spread from this book is closer to the 3:2 aspect ratio. Care needs to be taken when framing images for editorial work. The photographer has to be prepared to lose some of the visible image in the viewfinder if an editor wants to produce either a full-page or double-page spread from an image captured in a different aspect ratio. Many photographers instinctively design full frame. This can create difficulties when trying to crop the image to a different format.

Choosing a capture medium

There has been a shift towards digital image capture in recent years as it has the advantage of producing an image almost immediately (no processing required). It creates image files, downloaded to a computer, suitable for desktop publishing. A limiting factor has been the expense of digital cameras capable of providing the quality suitable for large commercial illustration.

Until recently commercial photography reproduced in magazines has traditionally and almost exclusively been produced using positive or reversal (transparency) film. The advantage of reversal over negative film has been that it is a one-step process to achieve a positive image. However, advances in digital capture are replacing film capture in most commercial situations. A negative film emulsion (still used extensively in the film industry) will give you, within its limitations, an image opposite to that seen through the viewfinder. It is only when a negative is printed that it becomes a positive image. The advantage of negative film is its greater 'latitude' and ability to handle higher subject contrast levels than positive film.

Image processing

Digital image processing is carried out on a computer platform. The commercial illustration industry favors Apple Macintosh computers and the software 'Adobe Photoshop'.

Color transparency film is processed using the E-6 process. This is a Kodak processing system and will process nearly all color positive films. Color negative film is processed using the C-41 process. This is also a Kodak processing system and will process nearly all color negative films. Color film processing should be undertaken by a professional laboratory. Although it is currently possible to purchase chemicals to process color film the money saved may well be a false economy when considering the experience and equipment required to produce consistent and accurate color processing.

The number of black and white processing systems are as varied as the number of films available. Although not covered in this book it is recommended all photographers develop a thorough understanding of black and white processing. It is relatively simple technology (it has changed little since its introduction) and easy to learn.

Appropriate exposure

Assessing correct image exposure can be achieved by viewing the film on a light box or by examining a histogram of the digital image file. It takes practice to be precise about the subtleties of underexposure and overexposure but there is a simple starting point. If there is no image detail something is wrong.

If, when viewing a digital image, a large peak is apparent at one or both ends of the histogram then detail may be missing through excessive contrast or poor exposure.

If negative film appears 'dense' (transmits very little light) with no visible detail it is probably overexposed. If positive film appears 'dense' it is probably underexposed.

If negative film appears 'thin' (transmits nearly all light) with no visible detail it is probably underexposed. If positive film appears 'thin' it is probably overexposed.

Positive image capture

Positive image capture can be further subdivided:

- ~ Digital capture
- ~ Professional or general purpose transparency film
- ~ Tungsten or daylight transparency film.

Digital capture

Digital capture has already impacted upon commercial photography. For many commercial photographers who have not yet started to capture digitally it is not a question of 'if', but 'when'. At the present time the hardware and software required for high resolution digital image capture is the more expensive option compared to the equivalent film capture, but for those photographers who require lower resolution images digital is usually the answer.

Professional film

Professional film is made to the highest quality-control procedures. The film material is more consistent between batches than the equivalent general purpose film and is essential when speed or color variations cannot be tolerated. Professional film should only be purchased if it has been stored in a refrigerator. The increased price for professional film is not warranted on many jobs that the photographer undertakes.

Tungsten and daylight

Tungsten film is only available as professional film and is distinguished by the letter 'T' after the ISO rating. It is available in three ISO ratings and is generally used for commercial studio applications. Many photographers refer to the film by its prefix letters, e.g. EPY, EPT and EPJ are current examples.

Most transparency film is balanced for daylight (5500K). Color film can only achieve correct color balance when it is used with the appropriate light source. It is possible, however, to achieve interesting results by using a film with an incorrect light source. If a daylight film is used with tungsten light a very warm sepia effect is obtained. If tungsten film is used with a daylight source a cold blue effect will be the result. In both cases the ISO will change, resulting in variations to exposure.

Tungsten

ISO	FORMAT	PROCESS
64	small, medium, large	E-6
160	small, medium	E-6
320	small	E-6

Daylight

ISO	FORMAT	PROCESS
64 & 100	small, medium, large	E-6
200	small	E-6
400	small, medium	E-6

www.kodak.com

Image characteristics

Capture mediums have the following characteristics:

- Sensitivity (speed)
- Sharpness (grain and/or resolution)
- Contrast
- Noise (digital sensors only).

Sensitivity

All films and image sensors are assigned an ISO (International Standards Organization) rating. This rating indicates its sensitivity to light. The higher the rating the greater the sensitivity. Most image sensors can be assigned different ratings as and when required.

Films are available from 50 ISO to 3200 ISO whilst image sensors are available that can be rated between 50 and 6400 ISO. Each time the ISO doubles the film or image sensor is twice as light sensitive, e.g. a 400 ISO film requires only half the exposure of a 200 film. The 400 film can therefore be said to be one stop faster than a 200 ISO film and two stops faster than a 100 ISO film. Films are often referred to as slow, medium or fast. A film is described as being slow if its ISO is 64 or less and fast if its ISO is 400 or more.

The advantage of using fast film or an image sensor rated at a high ISO is a photographer is able to use faster shutter speeds to either freeze action or avoid camera shake. The disadvantage of using faster film or an image sensor rated at a high ISO is its decreased resolution or sharpness (film only) and the increased size of film grain or digital 'noise'.

Sharpness

A digital image is made up of 'pixels' or picture elements whilst the silver image on film is made up from a grain pattern of silver halides. As a film's ISO increases the size of the grain increases whilst increased noise levels result from raising the ISO of an image sensor. The grain pattern or noise becomes apparent when the image is enlarged.

As the image is enlarged it appears progressively less sharp. An image created using slow speed film or a high resolution image sensor will enlarge to a greater physical size before the sharpness becomes unacceptable than if the same image was created using a fast speed film or lower resolution image sensor. Reduced grain size or low noise levels are strong selling points for fast films and high ISO image sensors.

Contrast

Digital image sensors have a 'latitude' similar to transparency film when shooting JPEGs in camera so great care must be taken to protect images from loss of detail resulting from excessive contrast. The photographer should save images using the Raw format in high-contrast situations. As the ISO rating of film increases the contrast decreases. The slower the film, the higher the contrast. As film is 'pushed', however (increasing the recommended film speed and processing time), the contrast increases. This is a result of the processing and not the film speed used for exposure. High-contrast film is not easy to use with high-contrast subject matter. If the photographer is not skilled with this combination, highlight and shadow information may be lost.

Noise

Sensors in the small pocket-sized digicams and fixed lens digital cameras are very small, whilst in DSLRs the sensor size is comparatively much larger (more than double the dimensions and quadruple the surface area in the case of 35mm DSLRs and 16 times the surface area in the case of medium-format digital sensors). The use of small sensors in prosumer digicams usually leads to increased levels of noise when compared to the images captured with a DSLR camera at the same ISO - especially when comparisons are made at higher ISO settings. Larger sensor sites typically lead to less problems with noise. Noise can be almost non-existent in images captured with medium-format digital cameras or professional 35mm DSLRs shooting at a very low ISO. In the consumer range of of DSLRs, cameras with a CMOS sensor rather than a CCD sensor tend to perform better at ISO settings over 400.

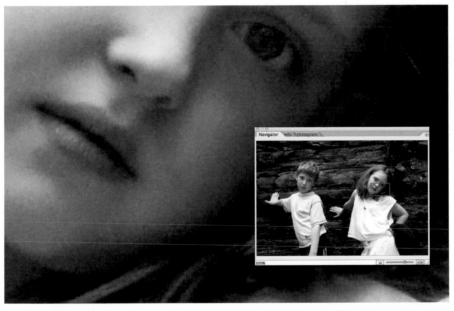

A small sensor pushes its luck at 400 ISO - image magnified to 300% (see inset)

If we examine the detail (zooming in to 200 or 300% on screen) from an image captured at ISO 400 on the Fuji fixed lens digicam (perhaps one of the better small sensors at high ISO speeeds) we will discover posterization and lumpy tones and smudged or blurry detail. These are evident as a result of in-camera processing in an attempt to suppress the noise that is inherent in files captured with the small sensors found in prosumer digicams. These degradation of image quality is also replicated when excessive noise reduction is used in post-production image-editing software.

This image processing makes the image look as if we are viewing the file through distorted glass. Quality is starting to be compromised. If we view a Raw file from a file that has been captured at 400 ISO without noise suppression then the smudged detail is replaced with luminance and color noise that is reminiscent of images captured with high-speed color film.

Note > Although the image artifacts that are starting to appear at 400 ISO, they are barely noticeable in a 4 x 6 inch print or small screen preview of the entire image.

Noise reduction and sharpening in Adobe software

Set the image to 100% and click on the Detail tab in your Adobe software to access the sharpness and noise reduction controls. The Luminance Smoothing and Color Noise Reduction sliders (designed to tackle the camera noise that occurs when the image sensors' ISO is high) should only be raised from 0 if you notice image artifacts such as noise appearing in the image window.

In the image above the sensor was set to 400 ISO on a budget DSLR. Both luminance noise (left) and color noise (right) are evident when the image is set to 100%. With more expensive DSLR cameras set to 100 ISO it is common to leave the Luminance slider set to 0.

Note > The Luminance Smoothing and Color Noise Reduction sliders can remove subtle detail and color information that may go unnoticed if the photographer is not careful to pay attention to the effects of these sliders. Zoom in to take a closer look, and unless you can see either the little white speckles or the color artifacts set these sliders to 0.

Limitations of film capture

Expiry date

At the time of manufacture all film products have an expiry date printed on their packaging. Do not use film once this date expires. The manufacturer will not guarantee correct rendition of color and reliable results cannot be predicted. Store unexposed film at a constant temperature, preferably in a refrigerator, but do not freeze.

Color temperature and white balance

It is not important to fully understand the theory of color temperature other than to know that capturing color images requires the correct match between capture medium and light source to avoid excessive color casts. Black and white film is relatively unaffected by color temperature although a small increase in exposure (as indicated by the MIE reading) is often required when using tungsten lights.

> **Tungsten film is rated at 3200K and used with tungsten lighting.**
> **Daylight film is rated at 5500K and used with flash and daylight.**

To render correct color, the use of a 'white balance' or filtration can be used to balance any image sensor or film to any lighting situation. The filtration required for film is listed in the manufacturer's specifications packaged with the film.

Reciprocity

Reciprocity, more correctly referred to as reciprocity failure, is a measure of the film's ability or inability to handle extreme exposure times. Reciprocity, in general terms, takes effect when shutter speeds are greater than 1 second when using daylight color film, greater than 30 seconds when using tungsten color film and 1 second when using black and white. All manufacturers issue a technical information sheet with their professional film packaging stating the reciprocity values relevant to that batch (manufacturing identification) of film. This should be followed closely.

Without going into the causes of reciprocity the remedy is to reduce shutter speed (time) and compensate by increasing aperture (intensity). Increasing exposure by increasing time will only compound the problem.

The results of not compensating for reciprocity is an underexposed image, varying shifts in color rendition and unpredictable results.

Activity 1

Photograph a subject of average contrast using the capture medium of your choosing.

Adjust shutter speed and the intensity of light so exposure times start at 1 second with the aperture at f2.8 or f4.

In one stop increments increase exposure time to 64 seconds.

Label the results for reference, comparison and discussion.

At what exposure time did the images suffer reciprocity failure or excessive levels of noise?

Latitude

Latitude is a measure of the ability or inability to record detail in subjects with extreme contrast and variation from correct exposure.

It is an accepted rule that most modern film emulsions and digital image sensors have an approximate five to seven stops latitude, although this is sure to increase as manufacturers develop new technology. This means that if you underexposed an 18% gray card by three stops it would appear black on the image. If you overexposed it by three stops it would appear white. The human eye has almost limitless latitude because of its ability to compensate for changes in contrast and light levels. Film and image sensors are incapable of doing this due to their limited latitude. Color transparency and most image sensors capturing in JPEG mode have a five stop latitude and can handle a contrast ratio of only 32:1 before loss of detail occurs. Black and white and color negative film have a latitude of seven stops and can handle a contrast ratio of 128:1 (this can be greater with medium-format digital sensors). The human eye is capable of adjusting to a ratio in excess of 1000:1.

Rodrick Bond

Activity 2

Choose a capture medium (digital, transparency or negative film).

Light a gray card with a diffuse light source; ensure the card fills the frame.

De-focus the camera and take a reflected or incident meter reading.

Either side of correct exposure, overexpose and underexpose in sequence one to five stops.

Process the film or download the digital files and open in Adobe Photoshop.

Evaluate and document the point at which the film or image sensor is unable to record detail above and below correct exposure (latitude).

This indicates the capture medium's latitude and its ability to handle incorrect exposure.

Pushing and pulling film

Photographers may push or pull film to alter the resulting contrast. A photographer may also have to push film on location when the ambient light is low. A safety net all photographers can use when using film is the manipulation of processing after exposure. This applies to all film materials. Despite the precision of the camera and metering systems used, human and equipment error can still occur when taking a photograph.

If the situation allows bracketing (exposure one and two stops either side of and including normal) is a way of ensuring correct exposure. When there is not the opportunity to bracket exposure and all exposures are meter-indicated exposure (MIE) it is advisable to clip test the film.

Clip test

Clip testing is a method of removing the first few frames from an exposed roll of film and processing as normal (i.e. to manufacturer's specifications). If these frames appear underexposed, a push process (over processing the film) may improve or compensate for any error in exposure. If overexposure is evident a pull process (under processing) may correct the result.

The amount of pushing or pulling required to produce an acceptable result is generally quantified in stops. If an image appears underexposed by one stop push the film one stop. If an image appears overexposed one stop pull the film one stop.

Push processing color transparency having correct exposure is also an option. It has the effect of cleaning up the highlights and giving an appearance of a slight increase in contrast. Pushing in excess of what would be required to achieve this can be an interesting exercise. The results can be unpredictably dramatic. Most professional film processing laboratories offer this service.

Normal process   *One stop push*
                                                        - Fabio Sarraff

Activity 3

Load a camera with color transparency.

Deliberately underexpose by one and two stops subjects with average contrast.

Clip test the film - normal process. Clip test again - one stop, two stop and three stop push.

Assess the result and process the rest of the film at processing levels you determine.

Cross-processing effect

Similar to over- and under-processing is the practice of processing a film in chemicals different to that suggested by the manufacturer.

If a transparency film normally processed E-6 is instead processed C-41 (color negative) the result is a negative that will print with colors and tones different to those originally photographed.

Matching a film to an incorrect process can be done in any combination but the results can vary from amazing to very disappointing, but well worth the experimentation.

It is important to note film speed changes when cross-processing. As a general rule transparency film should be underexposed by one stop when processing in C-41, and negative film overexposed by one stop. This is only a guide and variations in film speed and processing should be tested to obtain the result you want.

Digital cross-processing

Using the software Adobe Photoshop it is possible to create a visual equivalent of cross-processing using digital editing techniques.

Normal process

Cross-process
Michael Wennrich

Activity 4

Photograph subjects of varying contrast using transparency film or digital capture.

Bracket the exposures and keep a record of aperture and time if using film.

Use Adobe Photoshop to create the effect of cross-processing or process the film using the C-41 process (consult the lab prior to processing).

Label the results for reference, comparison and discussion.

Image preview
Polaroid

Since its introduction in 1946 Polaroid materials have become a common tool in the assessment of exposure, contrast, composition and design. To most people, whether it be the photographer, a client, an art director or someone wanting a family portrait it is the first evidence of the photographic process and an indicator of where improvements can be made. Polaroid has become 'the rough drawings' on the way to the final photograph.

All Polaroid materials, color or black and white, will give a positive image. In some cases a negative, as well as a positive, will be produced that can be printed in the normal way at a later date. When using Polaroid follow the instructions relating to film speed (ISO or ASA) closely and observe the processing times relating to room temperature. It is important processing times are followed carefully.

When assessing a Polaroid for exposure relative to another film type it should be realized more detail will be seen in a correctly exposed color transparency than will be seen in the Polaroid's positive reflection print. This is because transparencies are viewed by transmitted light and prints by reflected light. The Polaroid will appear 'thin' if it is overexposed and 'dense' if it is underexposed. Types of Polaroid film suitable for this subject are listed below.

TYPE	ISO	FORMAT
54 (b/w)	100	Large
55 (b/w-negative)	50	Large
59 (color)	80	Large
64 (color-tungsten)	64	Large
664 (b/w)	100	Medium
665 (b/w-negative)	80	Medium
690 (color)	100	Medium

www.polaroid.com

Digital display

Digital capture negates the use of Polaroid film as the image can either be reviewed on the camera's LCD or downloaded to a computer. The histogram can give detailed guidance as to exposure levels but photographers using the Raw file format need to be aware that the histogram on the camera's LCD is usually optimized for the JPEG file format (see Exposure and Light Meters > Reading exposure levels).

Activity 5

Either: establish an appropriate digital platform for previewing digital files.
Or: using a diffuse light source light a person's hand. Correctly expose (incident reading) onto Polaroid. Expose onto color film using Polaroid as your means of determining exposure and composition.

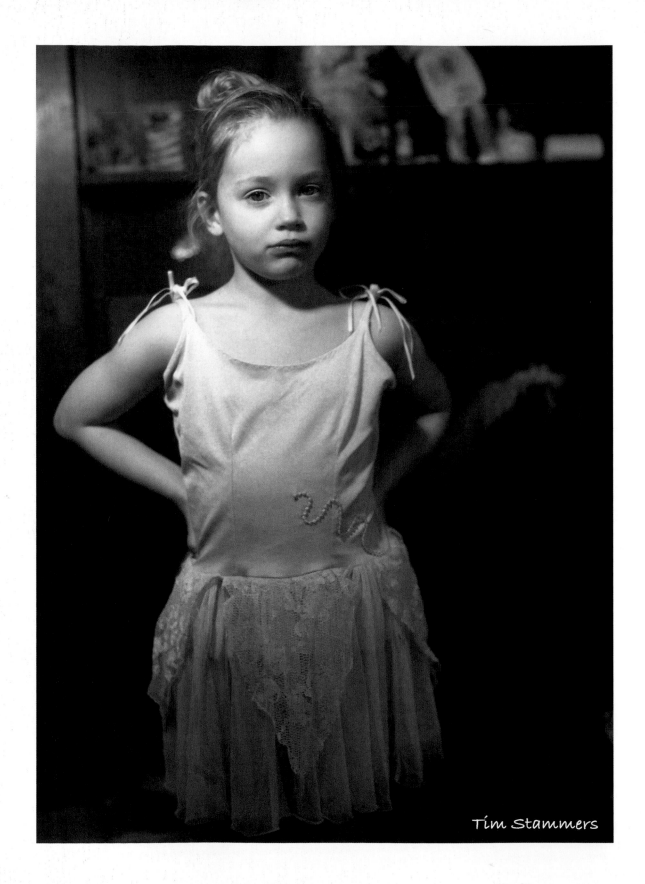

Tim Stammers

color correction and filtration

Itti Karuson

essential skills

~ Learn how to create an accurate white balance in camera and in post-production image editing.

~ Gain a working knowledge and understanding of photographic filters.

~ Gain an understanding of the appropriate application of filters to modify light for the purpose of appropriate exposure and visual effect.

~ Understand basics of color theory.

~ Document images illustrating different filtration techniques.

~ Create images using technique, observation and selection demonstrating a practical understanding of filtration.

Introduction

The purpose of a filter is to selectively modify the light used for exposure. Filters are regularly used by professional photographers. They are an indispensable means of controlling the variations in light the photographer is likely to encounter. The range of filters used varies according to the range of situations likely to be encountered. However, when capturing Raw file images it is possible to undertake color correction in camera or in post-production. See 'Characteristics of Light'.

Studio

In the studio the photographer is able to create images with a consistent quality using few, if any, filters. The photographer must simply ensure the film stock or image sensor white balance is carefully matched to the light source being used. The studio photographer has the option of filtering the light source, the camera lens or placing the filters between the lens and the image plane. If the photographer is using a mixture of light sources the photographer should ideally filter the light at its source. Any filter attached to the camera lens must be of premium quality - preferably glass.

Location

On location where ambient light is the primary light source or cannot be eliminated from the overall exposure the necessity to carry and use a broad range of filters increases.

If choosing to purchase filters for lenses the photographer needs to be aware of the thread size on the front of each lens intending to be used. Filter sizes for fixed focal length, wide-angle and standard lenses on 35mm and DSLR cameras are usually between 48 and 55mm. Medium-format, telephoto and zoom lenses may have thread sizes much larger. Purchasing every filter for every lens would be an expensive operation, so filters have to be selected carefully through actual rather than perceived need. Plastic filters are available from manufacturers such as 'Cokin' which can be adapted to fit a range of different lens diameters. The initial outlay to filter all lenses can be greatly reduced, but their working life may be far less due to the greater risk of damage.

Basic color theory

To be comfortable with filtration it helps to understand basic color theory. The broad spectrum of visible light is divided into three primary colors and three secondary colors. The primary colors of light are red, green and blue (RGB).

The secondary colors are yellow, cyan and magenta. When used in the printing industry to create images black is added (CMYK or four-color printing).

Each secondary color is a combination of two primary colors and is 'complementary' to the third primary.

- ~ Yellow is complementary to blue
- ~ Cyan is complementary to red
- ~ Magenta is complementary to green.

Color accuracy on screen

Straight out of the box just about all LCD monitors are too bright and too blue for photo editing (gray tones are not neutral), so we need to change them to settings that are commonly recognized as 'standard' for professional photographers. This process is called 'monitor calibration'. The next part of the process is to measure the color characteristics of your unique monitor so that Photoshop understands how color is displayed on your screen. The color characteristics are saved in a file called a 'color profile' that uses the file extension '.icc'. Photoshop can then read a monitor profile to ensure that images are displayed accurately on your screen. If the photographer only takes one action to improve their color management it would be to plant the cornerstone of color management - calibrate and profile the monitor you are working on. Photoshop will now display what your camera saw when you first captured the image. Any adjustments you now make to the color or tone of the image will be appropriate and not misguided due to a monitor that has not been calibrated and skews the colors so that they appear incorrect.

If you require a color critical workflow it is essential to create the optimum viewing conditions when working with digital images. Start by positioning your monitor so that it does not reflect windows or lights. Every commercial photographer must then calibrate and profile their monitor if color accuracy is important to their retouching workflow. The Industry standards are:

*   Whitepoint - D65
*   Gamma 2.2
*   Luminance between 100 and 140 cd/m^2

Note > A standard unit of measurement for luminance is often stated as candela per square metre or cd/m^2.

Budget devices are very affordable and easy to use (such as the Pantone Huey or Spyder2 Express). Professional quality but affordable units such as the X-Rite/Gretag Macbeth Eye-One Display 2 takes the guesswork out of monitor and room luminance levels.

Color profiles

Digital cameras tag each and every image captured with an image profile. This profile describes to the image-editing software the way the camera has interpreted and recorded the colors that it has captured. In this way the colors can be accurately displayed on your calibrated and profiled screen.

Choosing a color space for the capture device

Most DSLR cameras and some digicams allow the user to choose one of two profiles, Adobe RGB or sRGB. When capturing images in the Raw format it is the editing software that understands the color characteristics of the sensor you have been using. If scanning film the color characteristics of the scanning device need to be tagged to each and every image as a scanner profile.

Note > Adobe Camera Raw and Photoshop Lightroom may need updating to the current version or the latest plug-in to read the Raw files from a new digital camera.

Choosing a Working Space for Photoshop

Photoshop can work with a range of colors that is bigger than the color gamut of the monitor. To work with these additional colors that are out of the range of most monitors but may have been recorded by your digital sensor, Adobe uses a virtual space or 'working space' instead of a monitor space for editing digital images. This gives Photoshop the ability to edit more colors than you can see on your screen. When importing images into Photoshop you may like to convert the images to a working space that is optimized for either print or screen viewing. The choices are:

- Adobe RGB for print.
- sRGB for screen.
- ProPhoto for fine print (printing that makes use of an extended color gamut, e.g inkjet printers using more than six inks).

Note > In Photoshop Lightroom images are only tagged with a working space profile when they are exported or uploaded to the web.

Color accuracy in camera

Is the color of an image accurate just because the camera tags the image with a profile? Not necessarily. The color temperature of the light source may not match the white balance that has been set in the camera or the color temperature of the film that is being used (you would have to be exceptionally lucky for the daylight temperature of the film to match exactly the color temperature of the light source on location).

Mark Galer

Both of the images above were assigned a profile in the camera but were then assigned different white balance presets ('Shade' for the small inset image and 'Sunlight' for the larger main image). Auto white balance in the camera makes a guess at the color temperature from the range of colors it is presented with as the framing changes for each and every frame (variation can be the name of the game here as the precise recipe of colors being presented to the camera is constantly varying). Auto white balance is about as accurate at recording consistent colors as auto exposure is at recording the most appropriate exposure in all situations, i.e. not very. The colors in an image can only really be accurate if the photographer creates a manual white balance from a known value (a neutral tone) or creates a reference image of the color temperature of the light source.

Note > Auto white balance can be especially problematic when recording a series of images in JPEG mode. The colors will invariable shift slightly for each image in the series, e.g. this would be a major problem for a wedding photographer who notices the subtle tones in the wedding dress are shifting between each and every image because of an auto white balance setting rather than using a white balance preset or custom white balance setting.

Correcting White Balance in post-production

It is quick and easy to use the White Balance tool in the Adobe Camera Raw interface or Photoshop Lightroom to quickly color-correct Raw images by simply clicking on a neutral tone within the image to quickly set the correct color temperature and tint.

If the subject you wish to capture does not have an obvious neutral tone then you can introduce a neutral tone as reference point in the first image of the shoot. This will enable you to measure the precise temperature and tint required to color-correct all the other images that share the same lighting conditions.

In this image a white balance card (a 'WhiBal' is used in the image above) has been introduced into the image and then the White Balance tool is used to set accurate temperature and tint settings.

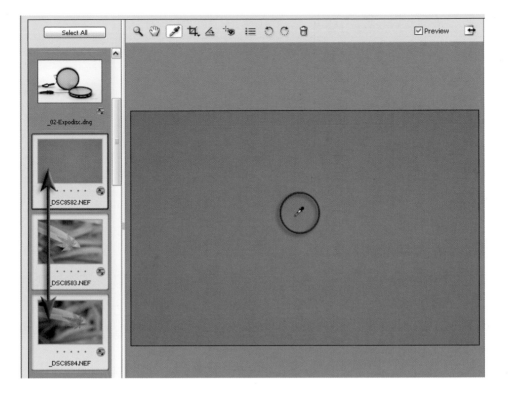

Click on the reference image thumbnail on the left-hand side of the Adobe Camera Raw interface. Then hold down the Shift key and click on the last thumbnail in the group of images that share the same lighting conditions. Select the White Balance tool and click on the main reference image preview to assign the correct white balance to all of the images.

This is before and after and clearly demonstrates how the Auto White Balance setting in the camera has misjudged the correct white balance for these images of Autumn leaves.

Note > The Expodisc can also be used create custom white balance settings in the camera, take accurate incident light meter readings and also help locate any dust on the camera's sensor (go to www.expodisc.com for more details about this useful product).

In some scenes there may be no neutral tones to click on and no opportunity to include a white balance reference card into the scene. In these instances it is important to either create a custom white balance setting in the camera at the time of capture, or capture a reference image using a product such as the 'Expodisc'. The Expodisc is placed in front of the lens and an image captured by pointing the camera back towards the light source (with the camera set to manual focus). The resulting image provides the photographer with a reference image that can be used to assign the correct white balance to all of the images captured in those lighting conditions.

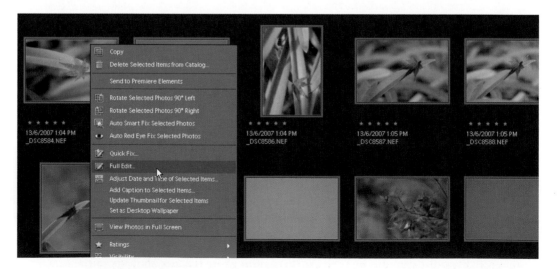

When you want to assign the correct white balance across a group of images in Adobe Camera Raw select multiple files in Bridge or Elements Organizer before opening.

PERFORMANCE TIP

So long as the photographer takes frequent reference images as the lighting conditions change, e.g. cloudy, sunny, time of day etc., color accuracy is assured with just a few clicks. Remember this color accuracy can only be fully appreciated if both the computer monitor and printer are calibrated to display accurate color.

Filters for lenses

Filters can be divided into five main categories:

- ~ Neutral filters
- ~ Black and white
- ~ Color conversion
- ~ Color balancing
- ~ Effects.

Neutral filters

A range of filters are manufactured that have little or no color. These include:

- ~ UV (haze) and 'skylight' filters (clear)
- ~ Neutral density filters (gray)
- ~ Polarizing filters (gray).

Mark Galer

UV and skylight filters

Ultraviolet (UV) radiation present in the spectrum of light is invisible to human vision but adds to the overall exposure of the image. It is most noticeable with landscape images taken at high altitude and seascapes. To ensure the problem is eliminated, UV filters can be attached to all lenses used on location. If the optical quality of the filter is good the filters may be left permanently attached to the lenses. The added benefit of this practice is the front lens element of each lens will be protected from scratching.

A skylight filter also eliminates UV light and has a color compensating effect. Shadows filled by skylight have a blue cast and the slightly pink filter helps to create shadows with a neutral color cast. Skylight filters are identified as a 1A and a stronger 1B.

Polarizing filters

Polarized light is the light reflected from non-metallic surfaces and parts of the blue sky. A polarizing filter can reduce this polarized light and the effects are visible when viewing the image in the camera.

A polarizing filter is gray in appearance and when sold for camera use consists of the actual filter mounted onto a second ring, thus allowing it to rotate when attached to the lens. The filter is simply turned until the desired effect is achieved.

The polarizing filter is used for the following reasons:

- ~ Reduces or removes reflections from surfaces
- ~ Darkens blue skies at a 90 degree angle to the sun
- ~ Increases color saturation.

Mark Galer

Possible problems

The filter should be removed when the effect is not required. If not removed the photographer will lose two stops and reduce the ability to achieve overall focus.

When the polarizing filter is used in conjunction with a wide-angle lens, any filter already in place should be removed. This will eliminate the problem of tunnel vision or clipped corners in the final image. Photographing landscapes when the sun is lower in the sky can result in an unnatural gradation, ranging from a deep blue sky on one side of the frame to a lighter blue sky on the other.

Activity 1

Create an image on a sunny day eliminating polarized light and one without using the filter.
Try to remove reflections from a shop window using a polarizing filter.
How effective is the filter at eliminating these reflections?
Compare and contrast your results with other students.

Neutral density filters

With manufacturers going to great lengths to create fast lenses with wide maximum apertures it may seem strange to find a range of filters available which reduce the amount of light at any given aperture. These are neutral density filters and are available in a range of densities. If only one is purchased the photographer should consider one that can reduce the light by at least two stops (four times less light). Neutral density filters are used for two reasons:

- ~ Reducing depth of field
- ~ Increasing duration of exposure.

Reducing depth of field

Very shallow depth of field is not always possible when working on location if the ambient light is very bright. If the photographer is using an ISO setting of 100 and direct sunlight to illuminate the subject the photographer may only be able to select f5.6 or f8 as their maximum aperture, if the maximum shutter speed available on the camera being used is 1/1000 or 1/500 second. This aperture may not be enough to sufficiently isolate the subject. If the aperture was increased further overexposure would result. The problem can be solved by using a lower ISO, a camera with a focal plane shutter capable of exceeding 1/1000 second, or a neutral density filter.

Duration of exposure - Martina Gemmola

Reduced depth of field - Samantha Everton

Increasing duration of exposure

Long exposures are not always possible when working on location if the ambient light is bright. If the photographer is using a film or image sensor at 100 ISO and direct sunlight to illuminate the subject the photographer may only be able to select 1/60 or 1/30 second as their slowest shutter speed, if the minimum aperture on the camera lens is f22 or f32. This shutter speed may not be sufficient to give the movement blur required. The problem can be solved by using a lower ISO, a lens with a minimum aperture smaller than f32 or a neutral density filter.

Black and white filters

When the photographer is using black and white film there is the option of controlling tonal values and contrast by using colored filters, e.g. a green apple and an orange may record on black and white film with the same tonal value or shade of gray. The use of an orange filter would result in the orange recording lighter and the apple darker; using a green filter would result in the apple recording lighter and the orange darker. Filters lighten their own color. In this way the tones are made different.

Many photographers using black and white film use a yellow/green filter as standard to correct the bias of the film towards the blue end of the spectrum.

The basic rule when using colored filters with black and white film is:

Adjacent colors are lightened.
Opposite colors are darkened.

Using the color wheel on the right, the photographer can quickly determine that colors the same as the filter and either side of the filter color will be lightened. All others will be darkened.

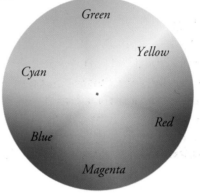

The color wheel

Black and white filters

Code	Color	Filter factor	Effect
Y2	Yellow	2	Reduces exposure of blue sky.
G	Green	4	As for Y2 plus lightens green foliage and renders good skin tones for daylight portraits.
YG	Yellow/Green	2	Corrects tones to that of human vision.
O2	Orange	4	Blue skies record as middle tones.
R2	Red	8	Creates dark and dramatic skies. Underexposes green foliage.

Activity 2

Using black and white film produce a landscape image using one of the filters from the 'Black and white filter chart' above.

Take a control image without the use of a filter for comparison.

Discuss your findings with other students.

Color conversion filters

The definition of a color conversion filter is one used to convert the color temperature of various light sources to match the color balance of the film being used. When capturing Raw file images it is possible to undertake color correction in post-production. See 'Characteristics of Light'.

Tungsten light

The filters used for this purpose are the 80 series including the 80A and 80B. These filters are blue in color and are used to balance daylight film with tungsten light sources. The 80B is used mainly in a studio situation to balance daylight film with photoflood bulbs specifically made for photographic lighting purposes.

	Daylight	3400K	3200K
Daylight film	None	80B	80A
Tungsten film	85B	81A	None

Color conversion chart

When using film a location photographer should have an 80A filter available. This filter allows daylight film to be used with tungsten-halogen lamps and record with approximately neutral tones. If daylight film is used in conjunction with an 80A filter and ordinary household light bulbs the resulting transparencies will still have a slightly warm cast.

A problem associated with using an 80A filter is the loss of two stops (filter factor 4). The photographer prepared for this will usually carry a 400 ISO film which they are prepared to push if necessary.

Fluorescent light

It is very difficult to assess the color cast that will result when fluorescent lights are illuminating the subject. Most images record with a green cast and most conversion filters are predominantly magenta colored with additional yellow or cyan filtration. An FLD filter is marketed for use with fluorescent lights and daylight film but it usually only improves rather than rectifies the situation.

With six main types of fluorescent lights commercially available all requiring different color conversions the best advice to a photographer is to:

Switch fluorescent lights off if possible.

Photographers leaving fluorescent lights on run the risk of a heavy color cast. This is often an oversight or the photographer may think the fluorescent lights are contributing little to the overall illumination and knowingly leave them on. The result is often devastating. Individuals with fair hair appear with bright green sprouting tufts from the tops of their heads and the tubes, if in the frame, appear as bright green.

Color balancing filters

Color balancing filters are used to produce more subtle changes in the color balance of the final image. They are particularly useful when working on location using color transparency film. The most common light-balancing filters used are the 81 and 82 series filters. The 81 series are warm in color (yellow) and the 82 series are cool in color (blue). The subtlest changes are made with the straight 81 or 82 filter, the A, B and C becoming progressively stronger. Exposure compensation is between one-third and two-thirds of one stop.

Warmer				Warm		Neutral	Cool		Cooler	
81EF	81D	81C	81B	81A	81	*	82	82A	82B	82C

One or two filters from the 81 series are particularly useful for removing the blue cast recorded when photographing in overcast conditions or in the shadows present in full sun. See the color correction chart in 'Characteristics of Light'.

Effects filters

Numerous special effects filters are available from camera stores. Most are a gimmick and once used are quickly discarded by the serious photographer. These include star-burst filters and graduated color filters.

Probably the most commercially viable special effects filter is the soft focus filter or diffuser. This is especially useful in close-up portraiture where the photographer wants to create a flattering portrait but the sitter has a somewhat less than perfect complexion.

Effects with standard colored filters

Many special effects can be created with conventional color filters and a little imagination. These include using a colored filter over the light source and a complementary filter on the camera lens. The effect is a neutral toned foreground with a background that bears the color cast of the filter on the camera lens.

Another effect is obtained by mounting a camera on a tripod and taking three exposures of moving subjects on the same piece of film. If the photographer uses a different primary colored filter (25 red, 61 green and 38A blue) for each of the exposures the effect is a near neutral background with colored moving subjects. Take a meter reading without the filters attached and open up one stop for each of the three exposures.

Activity 3

Create an image using an effects filter or filters. If you do not have access to an effects filter create your own using a piece of glass, Perspex or Gladwrap.

Place on the lens and alter the transmission of light by modifying the surface of the material chosen (smearing the glass or Perspex with Vaseline or stretching the Gladwrap).

Experiment and discuss your findings with other students.

Filter factors

Filter factors are indications of the increased exposure necessary to compensate for the density of the filter. A filter factor of two indicates the exposure should be doubled (an increase of one stop). A filter factor of four indicates the exposure should be increased four-fold (two stops) and eight requires three stops increased exposure.

Establishing an appropriate exposure

When using a camera with TTL metering the light meter is reading the reduced level of transmitted light and so theoretically the exposure should require no compensation by the photographer. In practice, when using the deeper color filters and TTL metering, it is advisable to take a meter reading before the filter is attached to the lens and then apply the filter factor. This leads to more accurate exposures being obtained as the meter can be misled by the colored light if metering through the filter.

Using more than one filter

Remove UV or skylight filters when using other filters. All filters provide UV filtration. Beware of vignetting or cropping the corners of the image when using multiple filter combinations. When using two filters the combined filter factors should be multiplied not added. If a neutral density filter with a filter factor of four is used in conjunction with an orange filter, also with a filter factor of four, the resulting filter factor would be sixteen, not eight. Adding the filter factors instead of multiplying them would lead to a one stop underexposure.

Filter factor table

Filter factor	Exposure increase in stops	Density*
1.25	$\frac{1}{3}$	0.1
1.5	$\frac{2}{3}$	0.2
2	1	0.3
2.5	$1\frac{1}{3}$	0.4
3	$1\frac{2}{3}$	0.5
4	2	0.6
5	$2\frac{1}{3}$	0.7
6	$2\frac{2}{3}$	0.8
8	3	0.9
10	$3\frac{1}{3}$	1.0
20	$6\frac{2}{3}$	2.0

* Note > The 'Density' of a filter is most often referred to when purchasing a neutral density filter such as an ND1 or ND2.

Rodrick Bond

Samantha Everton

skill ap

application module>>

digital
lighting on location

Mark Galer

essential skills

- ~ Change the character and mood of subject matter using lighting.
- ~ Develop an awareness of overall subject contrast and how this is translated by the capture medium.
- ~ Develop skills in controlling introduced lighting on location.
- ~ Research a range of fill and flash lighting techniques.
- ~ Produce photographic images demonstrating how lighting techniques control communication.

Introduction

The lighting in a particular location at any given time may not be conducive to the effect the photographer wishes to capture and the mood they wish to communicate. In these instances the photographer has to introduce additional lighting to modify or manipulate the ambient light present. In some instances the ambient light becomes secondary to the introduced light, or plays little or no part in the overall illumination of the subject. The following conditions may lead a photographer towards selecting additional lighting:

- The lighting may be too dull and the resulting slow shutter speeds would cause either camera shake or subject blur.
- Color temperature of artificial lights causing undesired color casts.
- The available light is leading to an unsuitable brightness range for the image sensor, e.g. the contrast is too high for the latitude of the capture medium and would lead to either overexposed highlights or underexposed shadows.
- The direction of the primary light source is giving unsuitable modelling for the subject, e.g. overhead lighting creating unsuitable shadows on a model's face.

James Newman

Activity 1

Select two images created on location where you feel the photographer has used additional lighting to the ambient light present.

Discuss why you think the lighting has been changed to suit the communication.

Fill

In high and extreme contrast scenes where the subject brightness range exceeds the latitude of the imaging sensor, it is possible for the photographer to lower the overall lighting ratio by supplying additional fill light. The two most popular techniques include using reflectors to bounce the harsh light source back towards the shadows or by the use of on-camera flash at reduced power output. Before the photographer jumps to the conclusion that all subjects illuminated by direct sunlight require fill, the photographer must first assess each scene for its actual brightness range. There can be no formula for assessing the degree of fill required when the subject is illuminated by direct sunlight. Formulas do not allow for random factors which are present in some situations but not in others. Photographers must, by experience, learn to judge a scene by its true tonal values and lighting intensity.

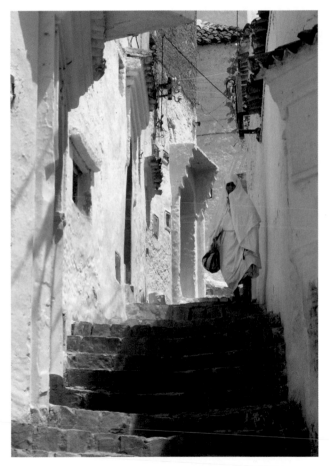

Mark Galer

The photograph above was taken in Morocco in harsh sunlight. The photographer could be mistaken for presuming this is a typical scene which would require fill light. If the scene is read carefully, however, the photographer would realize that the shadows are not as dark as one would presume. Meter readings taken in the shadows and highlights would reveal that the shadows are being filled by reflected light from the brightly painted walls.

Reflectors

Fill light can occur naturally by light bouncing off reflective surfaces within the scene. It can also be introduced by reflectors strategically placed by the photographer. This technique is often used to soften the harsh shadows cast on models in harsh sunlight.

The primary considerations for selecting a reflector are surface quality and size.

Natural fill - Mark Galer

Surface quality

Reflectors can be matt white, silver or gold depending on the characteristics and color of light required. A matt white surface provides diffused fill light whilst shiny surfaces, such as silver or gold, provide harsher and brighter fill light. Choosing a gold reflector will increase the warmth of the fill light and remove the blue cast present in shadows created by sunlight.

Size

Large areas to be filled require large reflectors. The popular range of reflectors available for photographers are collapsible and can be transported to the location in a carrying bag. A reflector requires a photographer's assistant to position the reflector for maximum effect. Beyond a certain size (the assistant's ability to hold onto the reflector on a windy day) reflectors are often not practical on location.

Activity 2

1. Select two examples where fill light has been used to soften the shadows created by a harsh direct light source. Comment on the likely source of the fill light used in each image.

2. Create an image by experimenting with different reflectors to obtain different qualities of fill light. Keep a record of the type of reflector used with each image and the distance of the reflector from the subject.

Flash

Flash is the term given for a pulse of very bright light of exceptionally short duration. The light emitted from a photographic flash unit is balanced to daylight and the duration of the flash is usually shorter than 1/500 second.

When the photographer requires additional light to supplement the daylight present flash is the most common source used by professional photographers. Although it can be used to great effect it is often seen as an incredibly difficult skill to master. It is perhaps the most common skill to remain elusive to photographers when working on location. Reviewing the image via the LCD screen will help the photographer master the skills more quickly. The flash is of such short duration that integrating flash with ambient light is a skill of previsualization and applied technique. The photographer is unable to make use of modelling lights that are used on studio flash units (modelling lights that can compete with the sun are not currently available). The skill is therefore mastered by a sound understanding of the characteristics of flashlight and experience through repeated application.

Flash, rather than reflectors, is used to preserve shadow detail - Shane Bell

Characteristics

Flash is a point light source used relatively close to the subject. The resulting light is very harsh and the effects of fall-off are often extreme (see page 15, 'Characteristics of Light > Intensity > Fall-off'). One of the skills of mastering flash photography is dealing with and disguising these characteristics that are often seen as professionally unacceptable.

Choice of flash

Choosing a flash unit for use on location may be decided on the basis of degree of sophistication, power, size and cost.

Most commercially available flash units are able to read the reflected light from their own flash during exposure. This feature allows the unit to extinguish or 'quench' the flash by a 'thyristor' switch when the subject has been sufficiently exposed. When using a unit capable of quenching its flash, subject distance does not have to be accurate as the duration of the flash is altered to suit. This allows the subject distance to vary within a given range without the photographer having to change the aperture set on the camera lens or the flash output. These sophisticated units are described as either 'automatic' or 'dedicated'.

ISO scale

Aperture scale

Distance range

Power setting

Control panel of an older style automatic flash unit

Automatic

An automatic flash unit uses a photocell mounted on the front of the unit to read the reflected light and operate an on-off switch of the fast-acting thyristor type. The metering system works independently of the camera's own metering system. If the flash unit is detached from the camera the photocell must remain pointing at the subject if the exposure is to be accurate.

Useful specifications

Perhaps the most important consideration when selecting an automatic flash unit is its ability to make use of a range of f-stops on the camera lens. Cheaper units may only have a choice of two f-stops whereas more sophisticated units will make use of at least four.

Ideally the output of a professional unit will have a high 'guide number' (an indication of the light output). The amount of time the unit takes to recharge is also a consideration. Many flash outfits have the option of being linked to a separate power pack so that the drain on the unit's smaller power supply (usually AA batteries) does not become a problem.

The flash head of a unit will ideally swivel and tilt, allowing the photographer to direct the flash at any white surface whilst still keeping the photocell pointed at the subject.

Dedicated

Dedicated flash units are often designed to work with specific cameras, e.g. Nikon 'speedlights' with Nikon cameras. The camera and flash communicate more information through additional electrical contacts in the mounting bracket of the unit. The TTL metering system of the camera is used to make the exposure reading instead of the photocell. In this way the exposure is more precise and allows the photographer the flexibility of using filters without having to alter the settings of the flash.

In addition to the TTL metering system the camera may communicate information such as the ISO of the capture medium and the focal length of the lens being used. This information may be automatically set, ensuring an accurate exposure and the correct spread of light.

Features such as automatic fill flash, slow sync, rear curtain slow sync, red eye reduction and strobe are common features of some sophisticated units. Often the manuals accompanying these units are as weighty as the manual for the camera which they are designed to work in conjunction with.

ISO

Focal length

TTL indicator

Distance range

Selected aperture

Control panel of a modern dedicated flash unit

Setting up a flash unit

- Check that the ISO has been set on either the flash or flash meter and the camera.
- Check that the flash is set to the same focal length as the lens. This may involve adjusting the head of the flash to ensure the correct spread of light.
- Check that the shutter speed on the camera is set to the correct speed (often slower than 1/250 second on a DSLR camera using a focal plane shutter).
- Check that the aperture on the camera lens matches that indicated on the flash unit. On dedicated units you may be required to set the aperture to an automatic position or the smallest aperture.
- Check that the subject is within range of the flash. On dedicated and automatic units the flash will only illuminate the subject correctly if the subject is within the two given distances indicated on the flash unit. If the flash is set incorrectly the subject may be overexposed if too close and underexposed if too far away. Check the accuracy of the flash output using a flash meter (see 'Guide numbers' in this chapter).

Guide numbers

Michael E. Stern, photographer and lecturer at Brooks Institute, talks us through the subject of guide numbers (GN) that are used to express the power of a class of electronic flash unit known as the speedlight. Speedlights are small flash units that work with DSLR 35mm cameras. Regardless of the stated guide numbers, professionals perform a guide number test to accurately measure and understand what the GN is for each speedlight unit and camera combination they work with.

Testing the guide number of a speedlight

The guide number calibration test is simple to perform and provides valuable information for photojournalists who routinely have to create images under difficult lighting conditions, and to help photographers in general who choose to make lighting ratios with multiple speedlight units. The GN formula and its two derivatives are as follows:

FSD (FSD = Flash to Subject Distance) x Aperture = GN

GN ÷ Aperture = FSD

GN ÷ FSD = Aperture.

The test is based on these parameters: the flash unit is set to full manual power and the zoom head is set to 50mm. The ISO is set to 100 and a camera sync speed of either 1/200, 1/250 or 1/500 second is selected. The FSD is set at ten feet exactly.

Testing the guide number of a speedlight - Michael E. Stern

The test

- Find a dimly lit room and position the flash exactly ten feet away from your subject wearing a white shirt (we don't want the ambient light contributing at all to the exposure value). For additional information have the subject holding either a gray card or a Macbeth Color checker. Double check the ambient light level by exposing a frame using the sync speed at f/8 (flash switched off). If the frame is black then the ambient light level is correct.
- Point the flash unit at the subject.
- Make a series of exposures beginning with f22 and ending with f8. Open up your aperture in 1/3 stop increments (you will have ten exposures when completed). Alter your exposures via the aperture and not the shutter speed.

Evaluating the results

Open up the two or three images in Photoshop that look correct in the sRGB or Adobe RGB (1998) working space. Set the color picker to a 3 x 3 or 5 x 5 average. Select the image with the best detail in the white shirt, i.e. the brightest highlights in the white shirt should fall between 240 and 250 to ensure that they print with detail. Evaluation of the subject's skin tone is also an important part of this measurement process. Skin tones vary so strive for a balance between 'white with detail' numbers and good skin tone values. It is highly recommended that a gray card or Macbeth Color checker be included as part of this test. Measure the gray card and look for a value of between 105 and 130. The precise number can vary due to inconsistencies in manufacturing of gray cards. If the gray card is not parallel to the camera the numbers can vary considerably. You'll have better luck with a Macbeth Color checker but make note that its middle gray is around 121 in the sRGB and Adobe RGB color spaces. As long as emphasis is placed on 'white with detail' numbers followed by skin tone and then middle gray values, an optimum exposure will be identified.

Finishing up

To better illustrate this concept, a frame will be selected and plugged into the formula. The frame captured using an aperture of f11 is selected as the optimum frame. It has white with detail and good skin tone values. An accurate GN for the particular flash unit and camera combination can now be established. It is 10 feet x f11 = a GN of 110 (FSD x Aperture = GN).

The photographer must now be comfortable with the implications of changing either the ISO on the camera or the FSD. If the ISO increases by one full stop from 100 to 200 then the aperture can also be adjusted one full stop to maintain an appropriate exposure, e.g. f11 to f16. This is known as equivalent exposures.

When the FSD changes the photographer divides the guide number by the distance to establish the most appropriate aperture to use. In our example, using the GN of 110, at just over 27 feet from the subject the photographer would have to use an aperture of f4 (GN ÷ FSD = Aperture) to maintain an appropriate exposure.

Flash as the primary light source

The direct use of flash as a professional light source is often seen as unacceptable due to its harsh qualities. The light creates dark shadows that border the subject, hot-spots in the image where the flash is directed back into the lens from reflective surfaces and 'red-eye'.

Red-eye

Red-eye is produced by illuminating the blood-filled retinas at the back of the subject's eyes with direct flash. The effect can be reduced by exposing the subject's eyes to a bright light prior to exposure ('red-eye reduction') or by increasing the angle between the subject, the camera lens and the flash unit. Red-eye is eliminated by moving closer or by increasing the distance of the flash unit from the camera lens. To do this the must be removed from the camera's hot shoe. This is called 'off-camera flash'. Red-eye can also be removed in post-production editing software.

Off-camera flash

Raising the flash unit above the camera has two advantages. The problem of red-eye is mostly eliminated. Shadows from the subject are also less noticeable.

When the flash unit is removed from the camera's hot shoe the flash is no longer synchronized with the opening of the shutter. In order for this synchronization to be maintained the camera and the flash need to be connected via a 'sync lead'.

For cameras that do not have a socket that will accept a sync lead a unit can be purchased which converts the hot shoe on the camera to a sync lead socket. If a dedicated flash unit is intended to be used in the dedicated mode a dedicated sync cable is required that communicates all the information between the flash and the camera. If this is unavailable the unit must be switched to either automatic or manual mode.

Keep the photocell of an automatic unit directed towards the subject during exposure.

Hot-spots

When working with direct flash the photographer should be aware of highly polished surfaces such as glass, mirrors, polished metal and wood. Standing at right angles to these surfaces will cause the flash to be directed back towards the cameras lens, creating a hot-spot. Whenever such a surface is encountered the photographer should move so that the flash is angled away from the camera. It is a little like playing billiards with light.

Activity 3

Connect a flash unit to your camera via a sync lead and set the unit to automatic.

Position your subject with their back to a white wall (within half a metre).

Hold the flash above the camera and directed towards the subject.

Make exposures at varying distances from the subject. Keep a record of the position of the flash and distance from the subject.

Repeat the exercise with the unit mounted on-camera.

Discuss the results of the most favourable image, commenting on the light quality, shadows and the presence of red-eye.

Diffusion and bounce

If the subject is close or the output of the flash unit is high, the photographer has the option of diffusing or bouncing the flash. This technique will soften the quality of the light but lower the maximum working distance.

Diffusion

Diffusion is affected by placing tissue, frosted plastic or a handkerchief over the flash head. Intensity of light is lowered but the quality of light is improved.
The flash can be further diffused by directing the flash towards a large, white piece of card attached to the flash head. Purpose-built attachments can be purchased.

A LumiQuest MidiBouncer

Bounce flash

The most subtle use of flash is achieved by directing the flash to a much larger, white reflective surface such as a ceiling for overhead lighting, or nearby wall for side lighting. This is called bouncing the flash. To obtain this effect the flash unit must have the ability to tilt or swivel its flash head. If this is not possible the flash can be removed from the hot shoe and connected to the camera via a sync lead. If an automatic flash is being used the photographer must ensure that the photocell is facing the subject when the flash is fired.

Activity 4

Create an image of a person using either diffused flash or bounce flash. For the bounce flash technique direct the flash towards a white ceiling or white reflector positioned to one side of the subject. Vary the distances of the reflector to the subject. Discuss and compare the quality of the light in your resulting image or images.

Note > Ensure the thyristor of the flash unit is directed towards your subject.
Alternatively use a flash meter to establish an appropriate exposure.

Fill flash

Fill flash can be a very useful way of lowering the brightness range. Often the photographer is unable to reposition the primary subject and the addition of fill light from the camera's position is essential to the image's success.

The aim of fill flash is to reveal detail in the dark shadows created by a harsh directional light source. The aim is not to overpower the existing ambient light and remove the shadows completely. If the power of the flash is too high the light will create its own shadows, creating an unnatural effect. Mount the flash unit on the camera's hot shoe and direct the flash towards the subject. To retain the effect of the primary (ambient) light source the flash is most commonly fired at half or quarter power. The ratio of ambient to flash light is therefore 2:1 or 4:1.

Manual - Select a smaller aperture on the camera from the one that is indicated by the flash unit or flash meter, e.g. if the meter or unit indicates f5.6 select f8 or f11 on the camera. Compensate for the reduced aperture by selecting a slower shutter speed on the camera so that the ambient light exposure is still appropriate for your subject. This action will lead to correctly exposing the ambient light and underexposing the light from the flash unit.

Automatic - Many automatic flash units have the facility to fire at 1/2 or 1/4 power, making fill flash a relatively simple procedure. If this facility is unavailable set the ISO on the flash unit to double or quadruple the actual speed of the ISO set in the camera to lower the output.

Dedicated - Many sophisticated cameras and dedicated flash units have a fill flash option. This should be regarded as a starting point only and further adjustments are usually required to perfect the technique. Power often needs to be further lowered for a more subtle fill-in technique. The photographer may also wish to select a 'slow-sync' option on the camera, if available, to avoid underexposing the ambient light in some situations.

Activity 5

Create an image using the fill flash technique.

Lower the lighting contrast of a portrait lit with harsh sunlight.

Experiment to see if you can lower the flash output on your unit to half or quarter power.

Discuss the light quality of the resulting image and the fill/ambient lighting ratio.

Flash as a key light

The main light in studio photography is often referred to as the 'key light'. Using studio techniques on location is popular in advertising and corporate photography where mood is created rather than accepted. In this instance flash becomes the dominant light source and the ambient light serves only as the fill light.

When the ambient light is flat, directional light can be provided by off-camera flash. This enables the photographer to create alternative moods. The use of off-camera flash requires either the use of a 'sync lead' or an infrared transmitting device on the camera.

Slave units

Professional quality flash units come equipped with a light-sensitive trigger (optical slave) so that as soon as another flash is fired by the camera the unconnected flash or 'slave' unit responds. On location the slave unit can be fired by the use of a low powered on-camera flash (optical slave), by radio communication (wireless) or infrared. Wireless offfers the most flexibility as line-of-sight is not required between the trigger and the slave unit.

Accessories

A tripod or assistant is required to either secure or direct the flash.
An umbrella or alternative means of diffusion for the flash may be considered.
Color compensating filters may also be considered for using over the flash head. A warming filter from the 81 series may be useful to create the warming effect of low sunlight.

Technique

- ~ Check the maximum working distance of the flash.
- ~ Ensure the key light is concealed within the image or out of frame.
- ~ Diffuse or bounce the key light where possible.
- ~ Consider the effects of fall-off.
- ~ Avoid positioning the key light too close.
- ~ Establish a lighting ratio between the key light and ambient light.
- ~ Consider the direction of shadows being cast from the key light.

When working at night the photographer may have the option of approaching the subject and firing a number of flashes manually during an extended exposure (recharging the unit each time). The photographer or assistant must take care not to illuminate themselves during this process.

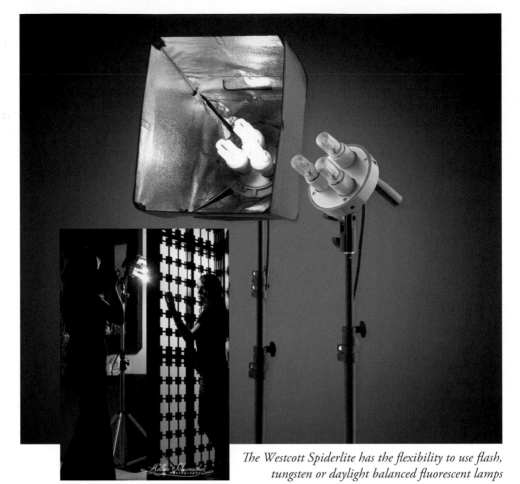

The Westcott Spiderlite has the flexibility to use flash, tungsten or daylight balanced fluorescent lamps

Halogen or daylight balanced fluorescent lamps on location

The availability of powerful tungsten halogen or daylight balanced fluorescent lamps (although not as powerful as flash) provides the photographer with a realistic alternative to using flash on location. The primary advantage to using tungsten halogen or daylight corrected fluorescent lamps instead of flash is that the light is constant, allowing the photographer to see the lighting effect as they move the light or lights into position.

Note > Although the modelling lights with studio style flash units may prove useful in a studio setting they are are usually rendered obsolete on location with the presence of brighter levels of ambient light.

Activity 6

Create an image using introduced light as a directional key light.

Make a record of the ambient exposure without the key light.

Discuss the effects of both the key and ambient light on your subject.

Slow-sync flash

Slow-sync flash is a technique where the freezing effect of the flash is mixed with a long ambient light exposure to create an image which is both sharp and blurred at the same time. Many modern cameras offer slow-sync flash as an option within the flash program but the effect can be achieved on any camera. The camera can be in semi-automatic or manual exposure mode. A shutter and aperture combination is needed that will result in subject blur and correct exposure of the ambient light and flash. To darken the background so that the frozen subject stands out more, the shutter speed can be increased over that recommended by the camera's light meter.

- Set the camera to a low ISO setting.
- Select a slow shutter speed to allow movement blur, e.g. 1/8 second.
- Take an ambient light meter reading and select the correct aperture.
- Set the flash unit to give a full exposure at the selected aperture.
- Pan or jiggle the camera during the long exposure.

Mark Galer

Possible difficulties

Limited choice of apertures - less expensive automatic flash units have a limited choice of apertures leading to a difficulty in obtaining a suitable exposure. More sophisticated units allow a broader choice, making the task of matching both exposures much simpler.

Ambient light too bright - if the photographer is unable to slow the shutter speed down sufficiently to create blur, a slower ISO should be used or the image created when the level of light is lower.

Activity 7

Create an image using the technique slow sync or flash blur.

Choose a subject and background with good color or tonal contrast.

Pan the camera during the exposure.

Discuss the results.

First exposure - exterior ambient light - exposure: MIE less 1/2 stop

Second exposure - total darkness - interior lights on - exposure: average highlights and shadows

Combined exposure

Double exposures

A double exposure can be used to balance the bright ambient light and the comparatively dim interior lighting of a building. Some digital cameras allow for the multiple exposures, that are required to achieve this outcome, to be recorded in-camera. If the camera does not allow for multiple exposures to be made using a single image file, two separate exposures can be combined in post-production. To achieve this result the photographer must use a tripod and take care not to disturb the alignment whilst adjusting the camera to make the second exposure. If the camera's white balance is set to daylight the interior lighting will record as a different color temperature to the exterior daylight. If the images are combined in post-production the interior lighting is placed on a layer above the exterior lighting layer. Set the interior lighting layer to the Lighten blend mode.

High dynamic range

Contrary to popular opinion - what you see is not what you always get. You may be able to see the detail in those dark shadows and bright highlights when the sun is shining - but can your film or image sensor? Contrast in a scene is often a photographer's worst enemy. Contrast is a sneak thief that steals away the detail in the highlights or shadows (sometimes both). A wedding photographer will deal with the problem by using fill flash to lower the subject contrast; commercial photographers diffuse their own light source or use additional fill lighting and check for missing detail using the 'Histogram' when shooting with a digital camera.

Combination of two exposures merged manully - Upper Yarra River by Mark Galer

Landscape photographers, however, have drawn the short straw when it comes to solving the contrast problem. For the landscape photographer there is no 'quick fix'. A reflector that can fill the shadows of the Grand Canyon has yet to be made and diffusing the sun's light is only going to happen if the clouds are prepared to play ball.

Ansel Adams (the famous landscape photographer) developed 'The Zone System' to deal with the high-contrast vistas he encountered in California. By careful exposure and processing he found he could extend the film's ability to record high-contrast landscapes and create a black and white print with full detail. Unlike film, however, the latitude of a digital imaging sensor (its ability to record a subject brightness range) is fixed. In this respect the sensor is a strait-jacket for our aims to create tonally rich images when the sun is shining - or is it?

Note > To exploit the full dynamic range that your image sensor is capable of, it is recommended that you capture in Raw mode. JPEG or TIFF processing in-camera may clip the shadow and highlight detail (see Adobe Camera Raw).

A single exposure in a high-contrast environment could result in a loss of detail in both the shadows and highlights, as can be seen by the tall spikes at Level 0 and Level 255 in the histogram of the image

If we can't fit all the goodies in one exposure, then we'll just have to take two or more. The idea is to montage, or blend, the best of both worlds (the light and dark side of the camera's not quite all seeing eye). To make the post-production easier the photographer needs to take a little care in the pre-production, i.e. mount the camera securely on a sturdy tripod. Take four exposures - two overexposing from the auto reading, and the other two underexposing from the auto reading. One or two stops either side of the meter-indicated exposure should cover most high-contrast situations.

Note > It is recommended that you use the shutter speed to bracket the exposures. This will ensure the depth of field is consistent between the different exposures.

Bracketing exposures

Setting your camera to 'auto bracket exposure mode' means that you don't have to touch the camera between the two exposures, thereby ensuring the first and second exposures can be exactly aligned with the minimum of fuss (the Auto-Align Layers feature in the full version of Photoshop does not work when your layers are Smart Objects). Use a remote release or the camera's timer to allow any camera vibration to settle. The only other movement to be aware of is something beyond your control. If there is a gale blowing (or even a moderate gust) you are not going to get the leaves on the trees to align perfectly in post-production. This also goes for fast-moving clouds and anything else that is likely to be zooming around in the fraction of a second between the first and second exposures.

Merge to HDR

Merge to HDR is a semi-automated feature in the full version of Photoshop for combining detail from a range of differnt exposures. A series of bracketed exposures can be selected and the Merge to HDR feature then aligns the images automatically. The Merge to HDR dialog box then opens and the user is invited to select a bit depth and a white point. It is recommended to save the file as a 32-bit image. This allows the exposure and gamma to be fine-tuned after the image is opened into Photoshop by going to Image > Adjustments > Exposure. As editing in 32 Bits/Channel is exceptionally limited the user will inevitably want to drop the bit depth to 16 or 8 Bits/Channel at some stage to make use of the full range of adjustment features.

When the Photoshop user converts an HDR 32-bit image to 16 or 8 Bits/Channel the user can choose a conversion method that allows the best tonal conversion for the job in hand. With very precise working methods HDR images can provide the professional photographer with a useful workflow to combat extreme contrast working environments. For situations where HDR is required but people or animals are likely to move between exposures a manual approach to merging the exposures is highly recommended.

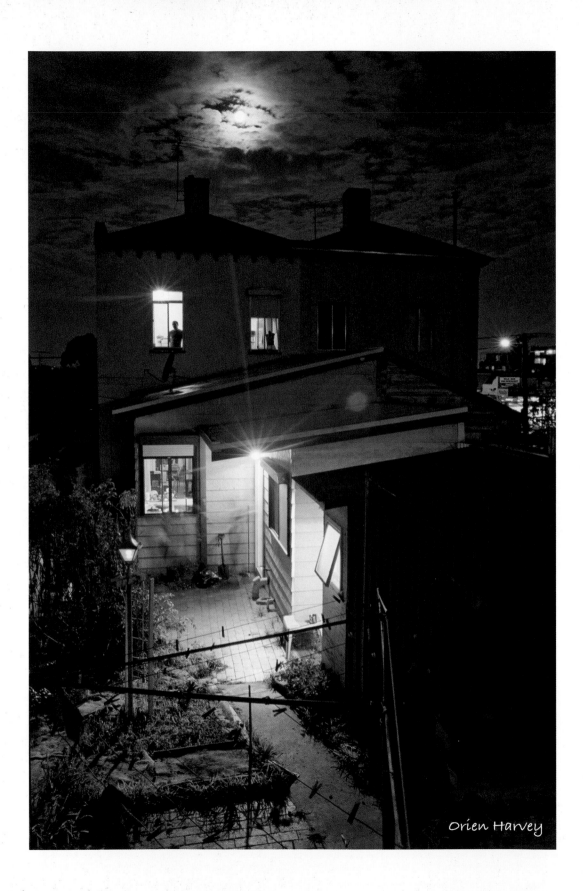

Orien Harvey

the zone system

Mark Galer

essential skills

~ Control the resulting tonal range of a black and white image using black and white film.

~ Learn to previsualize the printed image when viewing a scene.

~ Test the exposure index of the film you are using.

~ Test the accuracy of the development you are using.

~ Create images exposing for the shadows and processing for the highlights.

Introduction

The zone system is a technique of careful metering, exposure, processing and printing designed to give maximum control over the resulting tonal values of a black and white image that has been captured using black and white film. It is an appropriate technique to use on location where the ambient light cannot be altered to suit the contrast and tonal range desired by the photographer. It requires the use of short rolls of film or sheet film as the film processing has to be tailored to suit the subject contrast and lighting quality of each specific image.

The system was developed by the famous landscape photographer Ansel Adams. He formulated that just as an octave of audio frequency can be subdivided into notes from A to G#, the tonal range of the image (from black to white) can also be subdivided into tones or zones, each zone being one stop lighter or darker than the next. The zones on the photographic paper can be measured and are not open to interpretation. The zone system can, however, be used to interpret the subject differently depending on the desired outcome by the photographer. The photographer achieves this by choosing how dark or light the highlight and shadow tones will appear in the final printed image. 'Previsualization' is the term given to the skill of being able to see in the mind's eye the tonal range of the final print whilst viewing the subject. The zone system removes any surprise factor involved in the resulting tonal range of the image.

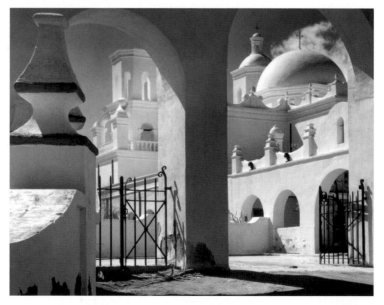

Arches - Ansel Adams © Ansel Adams Publishing Rights Trust/CORBIS

Benefits and limitations

With practice the photographer needs only to take one exposure to translate the subject into a preconceived image. Ansel Adams did not bracket his exposures. He did not need to. He knew precisely the result that each exposure would produce.

The time it takes to meter the subject carefully limits the use of the system. Images are created using the zone system, not captured. Henri Cartier-Bresson would not have found Ansel's zone system very useful for the images he wished to make.

Zone placement

Many photographers already use one aspect of the zone system when they take a light meter reading. Taking a reflected meter reading from a gray card and exposing the film to that meter indicated exposure is to place a tone (middle gray) to a specific zone (Zone V). The placing of a tone to a specific zone is called 'zone placement'.

To use the zone system fully the photographer must take two readings when metering the subject. One reading is taken from a highlight and one from a shadow. They are chosen by the photographer as the brightest and darkest tones which will require detail when these tones are viewed in the final image. These tones are selected subjectively. Each photographer may choose different highlight or shadow tones depending on the desired outcome. The selected highlight and shadow tones are then placed to appropriate zones.

0   I   II   III   IV   V   VI   VII   VIII   IX

The zone ruler

The tonal range of the print is of course much greater than just ten tones. Breaking the tonal range into ten precise zones allows the photographer to visualize how a metered tone in the subject will translate into a tone on the printing paper.

A selected tone can be moved up or down the scale one zone at a time simply by opening or closing the aperture one stop at a time. By placing a tone further up or down the scale the image is made darker or lighter as all other tones are moved in the same direction.

Activity 1

Frame a location (one that you can revisit again easily) when it is illuminated by directional sunlight. Approach a broad range of tones, from bright highlights to dark shadows, within the framed image and take a reflected light meter reading from each. Keep a record of each tone and its meter indicated exposure.

Take a gray card reading and bracket three exposures (meter indicated exposure, plus one stop and minus one stop). Process the film normally using the manufacturer's recommended development time, temperature and frequency of agitation.

Make a print from each of the three negatives without burning the highlights or dodging the shadows on medium-contrast printing paper. Using your notes label the range of tones you metered for in the first step of this activity, e.g. you may label a dark tone f4 @ 1/125 second and a highlight as f16 @ 1/125 second.

Discuss the tonal quality of each print with other students, e.g. can you see detail in the highlights and shadows?

Contrast control

The individual tones within the subject can be moved closer together (lowering the contrast) by reducing the processing time, or moved further apart (increasing the contrast) by increasing the processing time. Decreasing the processing time decreases the density of the highlights on the negative whilst leaving the shadow tones relatively unaffected. Increasing the processing time increases the density of the highlight tones on the negative whilst leaving the shadow tones relatively unaffected. There is some effect on the mid-tones in both instances but proportionally less than the highlights.

If shadows are missing from the negative (areas of clear film base within the frame) then no amount of extra development will reveal detail in these areas.

Negative with good detail *Contrast exceeding the latitude of the film*

Subject brightness range

The photographer can measure the contrast of the subject (subject brightness range) and then alter the processing of the negatives according to the desired contrast. The photographer exercises precise control by measuring the distance in stops between a highlight tone and shadow tone. If the distance between the selected highlight and shadow tones is greater than four stops (extreme contrast) processing can be decreased to lower the contrast of the image. If the distance between the selected highlight and shadow tones is less than four stops the processing can be increased to increase the contrast of the image.

Summary so far

- ~ The zone system is made up of ten major tones from black to white.
- ~ Each tone is one stop darker or lighter than the next.
- ~ Specific highlight and shadow tones of the subject are assigned to specific zones.
- ~ Zone placement of a shadow tone is a subjective decision. The decision dictates what detail is visible and how dark these shadows appear in the final image.
- ~ Development affects highlight tones proportionally more than shadow tones.
- ~ Increased or decreased processing time leads to increased or decreased contrast.
- ~ Subject contrast is measured in stops.
- ~ Shadow tones are controlled by exposure and highlight tones by development.

The zones

Each zone in the final image can be identified by its tone and the detail it reveals.
To obtain accuracy we must become familiar with the characteristics of each zone.

 Zone IX. Paper white. The standard print utilizing a full tonal range uses little or no paper white in the image.

Zone VIII. White without detail. The brightest highlights in the image are usually printed to this zone.

Zone VII. Bright highlights with visible detail or texture. If highlight detail is required it is placed in this zone by calculated processing time.

 Zone VI. Light gray. Caucasian skin facing the light source is usually printed as Zone VI.

Zone V. Mid-gray with 18% reflectance. A meter indicated exposure from a single tone will produce this tone as a Zone V on the negative.

 Zone IV. Dark gray.
Shadows on Caucasian skin are usually printed as Zone IV.

Zone III. Dark shadow with full detail and texture. If shadow detail is required it is placed in this zone by calculated exposure.

Zone II.
Shadow without detail.

Zone I.
Black.

Zone O.
Maximum black and is indistinguishable from Zone I in the printed image.

Activity 2

Refer back to the three prints created for Activity 1.

Select the image with the broadest range of tones (best exposure).

Label this image with the zones from I to IX. Use the description of each zone on this page to help you identify each zone.

Compare and discuss your labelled image with those of other students.

Zone recognition

Using the description in the previous section we are now able to recognize what each zone looks like in the printed image. Zones III and VII are of particular interest as they will indicate the accuracy of how a photographer has utilized the zone system. Important areas of shadow and highlight detail will have been preserved whilst still utilizing Zones II and VIII to give the print both depth and volume.

Zone III

Zone VII

Dark shadow with full detail and texture. If shadow detail is required it is placed in this zone by calculated exposure.

Bright highlights with visible detail or texture. If highlight detail is required it is placed in this zone by calculated processing time.

Operating the system

Gaining maximum control over the system requires practice. The student should take notes and compare the results with the actions taken. Mistakes may be made initially but these mistakes will lead to a greater understanding of the system.

Testing the accuracy of exposure and negative processing is crucial to obtaining precise control over the zone system. The photographer is advised to limit the combined choice of camera, light meter, film, developer, enlarger and printing paper until this control has been achieved, otherwise variations in outcome are inevitable.

Jana Liebenstein

Choice of camera, light meter and film

Use a camera and a light meter that provide accurate exposures. If the camera or meter receives a shock through impact, the equipment should be checked. Some retail outlets will offer to test the accuracy of the equipment.

Select only one type of 100 ISO film until control has been achieved. The student should ideally have some experience of processing this film prior to using it for the zone system. Establish an 'exposure index' for the film (see activity below). The usable speed for the film may vary from the manufacturer's recommended speed due to a variety of reasons.

Activity 3

Using black and white negative film, take several exposures of a subject with a four stop range. Someone wearing a white shirt with dark trousers or jacket would be ideal. Calibrate the exposure using a reflected light meter reading taken from a gray card. The subject should be illuminated with diffused light (cloud cover or shade). Bracket the exposures (1/3 stop intervals) keeping a precise record of each frame.

Process the negatives according to the manufacturer's specifications.

View the negatives on a light box and choose the best exposure with the assistance of an experienced practitioner. The darkest tones of the subject should render full texture and detail (no area of the image should appear clear).

Choose the best exposure and check your records to find the degree of compensation required. For example, if the best exposure for accurately rendering shadow detail is 2/3 stop more than the manufacturer's recommendation of 100 ISO then proceed to rate the film at 2/3 stop less, i.e. 64 ISO.

Exposure and processing

The zone system can be approached in a series of sequential steps. The entire system can be divided into two main practical skills. These are:

- Exposing for the shadows.
- Processing for the highlights.

Exposing for the shadows

View the subject and choose the dark shadows that you want to be able to see full detail and texture in when you view the final image. Take a specific reflected light meter reading from one of these dark shadow tones. Use a hand-held meter at close range or fill the frame of a 35mm SLR with the selected tone. Use a spot meter to isolate a tone from a distance.

Place the shadow tone in Zone III by stopping down two stops from your meter indicated exposure or MIE (e.g. if the light meter reading of the shadow tone is f4 @ 1/125 second then the final exposure could be f8 @ 1/125 second). This action is called 'exposing for the shadows'.

Metering for the shadows and processing for the highlights

Processing for the highlights

View the subject and choose the bright highlights that you want to be able to see full detail and texture in when you view the final image. Take a specific reflected light meter reading from one of these bright highlights. Measure how many stops brighter the highlights are than the shadows metered for in the previous step. If the shadow tone meter reading was f4 @ 1/125 the highlight tone may measure f16 @ 1/125 (four stops difference).

For bright highlights to record as bright highlights with full detail and texture they must fall in Zone VII (four stops brighter than the shadows). If this is the case the negatives can be processed normally. If the highlights measure more or less than four stops, decrease or increase processing time accordingly (see 'Compression' and 'Expansion').

Adjusting the development time

It is recommended that 'one shot' development (tank development using freshly prepared developer which is discarded after the film is processed) is used in conjunction with a standard developer. Developers such as D-76 and ID-11 are ideal for this test.

The student should use the same thermometer of known accuracy (check it periodically with several others) and adhere to the recommended development times, temperatures and agitation. A pre-wash is recommended to maintain consistency.

Viewing the negatives - the highlights of a high-contrast subject should be dark but not dense when the negatives are viewed on a light box. Newspaper print slid underneath the negatives should easily be read through the darkest tones of the image. Manufacturer's numbers and identifying marks on pre-loaded film should appear dark but not swollen or 'woolly'. The student should view the negatives in the presence of an experienced practitioner to obtain feedback.

Compression

If the selected highlights measure five or six stops brighter than the shadows placed in Zone III they will fall in Zone VIII or IX respectively. No detail will be visible by processing and printing the negative normally. The highlight tones selected can be moved one or two zones down the scale to Zone VII by decreasing the processing time. This situation is often experienced with a high to extreme subject brightness range (SBR).

Moving the highlights one zone down the scale is referred to as N−1, moving the highlights two zones down the scale is referred to as N−2. N−1 negatives are processed for approximately 85% of the normal processing time, N−2 negatives for approximately 75% of the normal processing time when using 100 ISO film. The action of moving highlight tones down the zone scale is called 'compaction' or 'compression'. Shadow tones remain largely unaffected by reduced processing time so the final effect is to lower the contrast of the final negative.

Expansion

If the selected highlights measure only two or three stops brighter than the shadows they will fall in Zone V or VI respectively. Highlights will appear dull or gray if the negatives are processed and printed normally. The highlight tones selected can be moved one or two zones up the scale to Zone VII by increasing the processing time. This situation is often experienced with a low SBR or flat light.

Moving the highlights one zone up the scale is referred to as N+1, moving the highlights two zones up the scale is referred to as N+2. N+1 negatives are processed for approximately 130% of the normal processing time, N+2 negatives for approximately 150% of the normal processing time when using 100 ISO film. The action of moving highlight tones up the zone scale is called 'expansion'. Shadow tones remain largely unaffected by increasing the processing time so the final effect is to increase the contrast of the final negative.

Calibration tests

The following additional tests can be conducted to check the accuracy of exposure and processing time.

Note > Changing printing papers or type of enlarger (diffusion or condenser) will change the tonal range and contrast that can be expected and so therefore should be avoided.

Exposure

The exposure index is calibrated by checking the accuracy of shadow tones on the negative. This can be achieved by using a 'densitometer' or by conducting the following clip test.

- Underexpose a gray card by three stops (Zone II).
- Leave the adjacent frame unexposed.
- Process the negatives according to the manufacturer's specifications.
- Place half of each frame (unexposed and Zone II) in a negative carrier.

- Make a step test using a normal contrast filter or grade two paper.
- Establish the minimum time to achieve maximum black (MTMB).
- The tone alongside the MTMB should appear as Zone II (nearly black).

MTMB Zone II

If the adjacent tone to the MTMB exposure on the test strip is too light (dark gray), decrease the exposure of the film. If the adjacent tone to the MTMB exposure on the test strip is too dark (black), increase the processing time.

Processing

Processing is calibrated by checking the accuracy of the highlight tones on the negative. This can be achieved by using a 'densitometer' or by conducting the following clip test.

- Overexpose a gray card by three stops (Zone VIII).
- Leave the adjacent frame unexposed.
- Process the negatives according to the manufacturer's specifications.
- Place half of each frame (unexposed and Zone VIII) in a negative carrier.

- Make a step test using a normal contrast filter or grade two paper.
- Establish the minimum time to achieve maximum black (MTMB).
- The tone alongside the MTMB should appear as Zone VIII (light tone).

MTMB 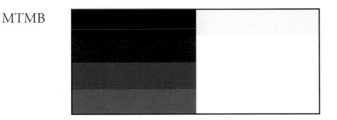 Zone VIII

If the adjacent tone to the MTMB exposure on the test strip is too light (paper white), decrease the processing time of the film. If the adjacent tone to the MTMB exposure on the test strip is too dark (Zone VII), increase the processing time.

Activity 4

Choose a 100 and 400 ISO film and conduct the exposure and processing tests as outlined on these pages.
Discuss your findings with other students.

Perfecting the system

For accurate previsualization the photographer must be familiar with all the materials and equipment in the chain of image creation. A common mistake is choosing a few very dark shadows to place in Zone III and the brightest highlights to place in Zone VII. The result may be a flat low-contrast image with the majority of the image placed in only three zones. Each time the system is operated the individual's ability to accurately previsualize the outcome improves.

Summary

- Take a reflected meter reading of a shadow tone.
- Place in Zone III by closing down two stops.
- Take a reflected meter reading of a highlight tone.
- Calculate how many stops brighter the highlight is than the shadow.
- Calculate the processing time using the information below.

Average processing adjustments for 100 ISO film

Contrast	Processing time %	
Highlight 6 stops brighter than Zone III	N+2	75
Highlight 5 stops brighter than Zone III	N+1	85
Highlight 3 stops brighter than Zone III	N−1	130
Highlight 2 stops brighter than Zone III	N−2	150

Activity 5

Revisit the location you photographed in Activity 1 at the same time of day with the same lighting (directional sunlight required).

Using the zone system create an image with a full tonal range.

Choose the shadow and highlight details you wish to place in Zone III and Zone VIII.

Expose, process and print the negative to obtain the final image.

Compare the results achieved in this activity with the image created for Activity 1 and discuss the visual qualities with other students.

A black and white digital workflow

It is possible to create high quality black and white images using a digital workflow as well as the more traditional analog film and photographic paper route. Just as the Zone System is about tonal control and manipulation we can exercise the same degree of precise control over digital tones or levels destined to be printed via an inkjet printer. This control can be exercised during the capture, post-production editing and printing stages of the digital process.

Capturing in RGB

It is important to capture the images destined for black and white as color images in the digital camera you are using. Do not be tempted to select any black and white option that may exist in your camera's preferences. It is advisable to capture your images using the Raw file format to access the higher bit depth and higher dynamic range that the Raw file format offers. Make sure you have read the section 'Raw format exposure considerations' in the chapter 'Exposure and Light Meters' (pages 51 to 58). To achieve rich shadow tones it will be important not to underexpose the shadow tones during the capture stage of the process.

Converting to grayscale in the editing software

The best place to convert a digital image from color to black and white (grayscale) is in Adobe Camera Raw or Photoshop Lightroom. Use the sliders in the HSL/Grayscale tab to fine-tune the conversion process. Dragging the red slider to the right will lighten the red colors in the image whilst dragging the blue slider to the left will darken the blue tones. You can then lower the exposure and increase the overall contrast using the tone curve controls to increase the drama further if required. For users of Photoshop Elements it is recommended that you open the image as a 16 Bits/Channel file from Adobe Camera Raw and then make use of the 'Convert to Black and White' adjustment feature to achieve maximum quality.

Black and white printing using an inkjet printer

If you hope to create neutral black and white prints from a color inkjet printer it is important
to either profile your printer or consider purchasing a printer that utilizes a gray ink cartridge
in addition to the black ink cartridge that is part of the overall ink set. Budget 8 x10 inch (A4)
printers usually struggle to print black and white images without a color cast in both the shadow
and the highlight tones. The 'canned' profiles that come shipped with these printers rarely produce
acceptable results. Attempting to print black and white images using the 'black' option in the
printer driver can result in unsightly ink dots in the highlights of the print and the image does not
match the luminance values of the calibrated on-screen display in your editing software.

Profiling an inkjet printer

A calibration device such as the Gretag Macbeth Eye-One Pro from X-Rite is capable of
creating a custom profile for your unique printer/ink paper combination. Alternatively you
can contact a profile service provider who can create a profile for you using the same hardware.
This involves measuring a target print from your printer to create a unique profile for the
color characteristics of your printer setup. Normally these profiles are created using no color
management as the untagged target file moves through the editing software and the printer
driver software. The file is opened in the editing software without converting to the working
space ('Leave as is'), 'No Color Management' or 'Same as Source' is then selected in the 'Print'
dialog box and the color management is switched off in the printer driver. To create a more
efficient profile for a budget printer it is recommended that the color management is left on
in the printer driver (the rest of the workflow remains the same). It is important to select a
standard color setting in the Color Controls of the printer driver with a Gamma of 1.8, if
available. This last step will ensure the shadow tones print with rich detail instead of printing
too dark (as is the case with standard profiles created for these budget printers).

**Note > The larger 13 x 19 inch (A3) printers using the higher quality inksets (such as
the Epson 2400 using UltraChrome K3 inks) have better 'off-the-shelf' performance for
printing black and white prints with better shadow detail.**

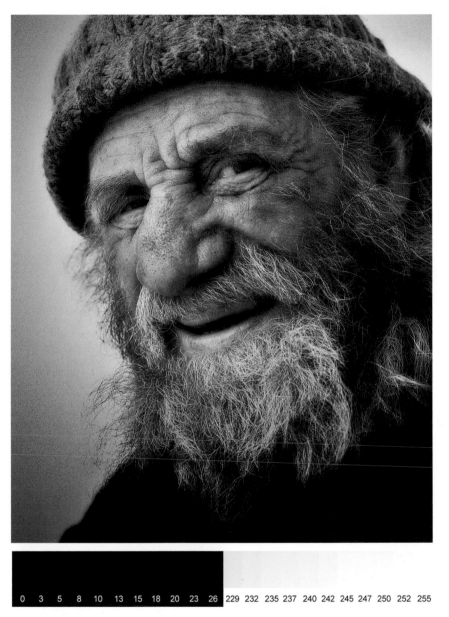

| 0 | 3 | 5 | 8 | 10 | 13 | 15 | 18 | 20 | 23 | 26 | 229 | 232 | 235 | 237 | 240 | 242 | 245 | 247 | 250 | 252 | 255 |

Target tones

With an accurate printer profile optimized for your printer you should be able to target the three most important tones in the Zone System. This is Level 110 which should print approximately the same tone as a photographers' gray card, the darkest shadow tone that is not black (Zone II) and the brightest tone that is not paper white (Zone VIII). Print a step wedge with tones of a known value so that you can accurately assess the performance of your printer, when working with a particular paper and ink combination. Once these values have been targeted in the print you can then accurately target these tones when working with images in your image-editing software (see the texts *Photoshop: Essential Skills* or *Adobe Photoshop Elements Maximum Performance* for more information on these post-production skills).

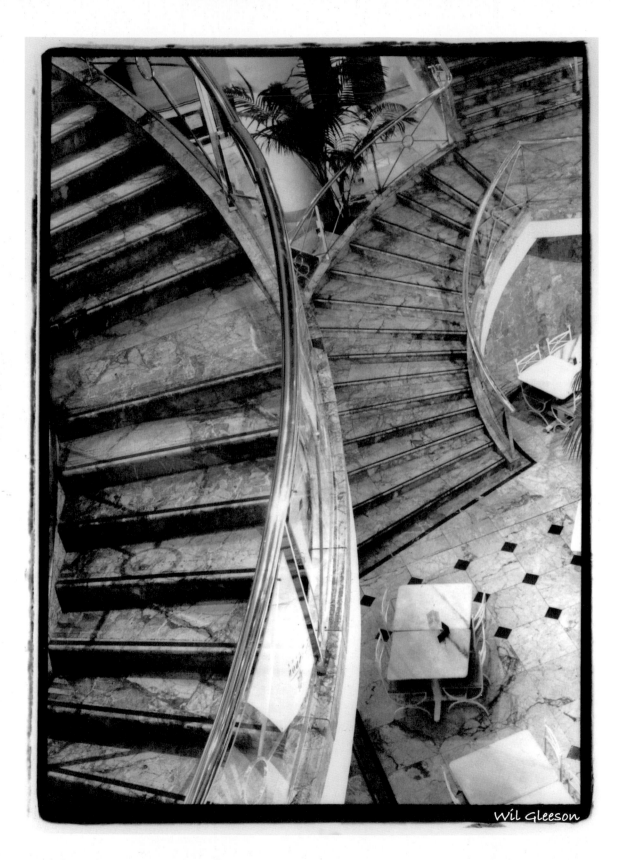

Wil Gleeson

studio lighting

Rodrick Bond

essential skills

~ Develop knowledge and understanding of the use of artificial light sources, camera and associated equipment in a studio environment.

~ Develop an awareness of the effect of artificial light in the creation and control of lighting ratios, shadows, contrast and exposure.

~ Observe the importance of lighting in the production of photographic images.

~ Produce photographs demonstrating a practical knowledge of the use of light.

~ Compile information relevant to the technique and production of each image.

Introduction

This study guide should be used as a practical source of information to understanding the use of tungsten light and flash in a studio situation. The explanation of how to use the two main light source configurations (floodlight and spotlight) is directly related to providing practical lighting solutions to the activities. It will also provide a basis for completion of the structured assignments in *Essential Skills: Studio Photography*. It is advisable that the technique and lighting approach suggested in each activity be initially followed and then adapted to individual subject matter.

Daniel Tückmantel

Approach

The sun, the dominant light source in the world outside the studio, is the starting point to understanding studio lighting. As you progress through your photographic career other approaches will inevitably influence you but an understanding of how to use a single light source to achieve many varied results is a discipline worth mastering. Try not to attempt too much too soon. Set yourself goals you know you can achieve within your limitations. Aspiring photographers may never have enough time or money but admirably they are exploding with ideas. It is making these ideas work within these constraints and abilities that will give successful results. Set out to achieve what you know is possible, take as much time as is available and exercise patience. When you think you have completed the photograph experiment with variations. Every time you move a light or alter its quality you will learn something. You will never take the perfect photograph. If you ever think you have, change careers because photographically the learning process has ceased.

Studio lighting

In a photographic studio all light is created by the photographer. An artificial light source can be anything from a large 20kW tungsten lamp to a single candle. These light sources fall into four main categories:

- Photoflood
- Tungsten-halogen
- AC discharge
- Flash.

Photoflood (3400K)

The photoflood is similar in design to the normal domestic light globe. It is balanced to tungsten and normally used without correction. If balanced to daylight an orange color cast will be evident. This can be corrected with the use of a blue (80B) filter or saving to Raw format. As the name implies this type of lamp is used when a broad, soft light source is required.

Tungsten-halogen (3200K)

The most commonly used photographic artificial light. Light is emitted as the element inside the glass envelope is heated and provides a continuous source of light. All tungsten light forms emit a great deal of heat when operating. It is balanced to tungsten and normally used without correction. If balanced to daylight an orange color cast will be evident. This can be corrected with the use of a blue (80A) filter or saving to Raw format. These lamps are mainly used where a point source of light is required (spotlight).

AC discharge (5600K)

Referred to as HMIs, AC discharge lamps have a very high output but emit less heat than tungsten when operating. They will maintain correct color balance throughout the life of the lamp and will render correct color when balanced to daylight. When balanced to tungsten an orange (85B) filter is required to remove the excess blue cast these lights emit or by saving to Raw format. HMIs are used predominantly in the film industry and in studio car photography.

Flash (5800K)

Flash is a generic term referring to an artificial light source of high intensity and short duration. It will render correct color when balanced to daylight. When balanced to tungsten an orange filter (85B) would be required to remove the blue cast. There is minimal heat output, and it maintains constant color balance and intensity. To assess the direction and quality of the light flash heads have built-in tungsten modelling lamps. As the output and intensity of the flash is far greater than the modelling lamps, exposure times will be too short for any tungsten exposure to register.

Health and safety
Power supply

It cannot be stressed strongly enough that the lighting equipment and studio power supply be either installed, or checked in the case of existing supply, by a qualified and licensed electrician. Without question working with powered light sources is the most dangerous part of a photographer's job. As a photographer it is inevitable light sources are taken for granted and unfortunately familiarity leads to complacency and poor safety practices.

- Electricity is dangerous. It can kill you.
- Never attempt to repair lights or wiring unless you are absolutely confident you know what you are doing.
- Always turn off the power and disconnect the cable before changing a globe.
- Never touch any part of a light or cable with wet hands.
- Exercise extreme care when photographing liquids.
- Always turn off the power to the flash pack when changing flash head outlets.
- Always be cautious when moving or connecting lights.
- Never use liquids near electricity.
- Use heat-resistant gloves when handling tungsten lights.
- Wear shoes with rubber soles.
- Ensure you know where and how to use the first aid kit.
- Ensure you know where and how to use the fire extinguisher.
- Ensure you are aware of emergency procedures related to work area.
- Ensure adequate ventilation of the studio area.

Hayley Sparks

Light sources
Tungsten

Vacuum tungsten lamps are widely used forms of artificial lighting in photography, film and television. They have a color temperature between 3200K and 3400K. Despite the extensive use of flash in a commercial studio, prior to any flash exposure the way a subject is lit is determined by the tungsten modelling lamps built into the flash heads. Flash gives a much shorter exposure time and a comparable quality of light to tungsten. It should be taken into account when learning the use of tungsten light that all film and television lighting is tungsten based. Generally they all fall into two major categories, floodlight and spotlight.

Floodlight

A floodlight produces a spread of light across a subject. The light from the globe bounces off the reflector in which it sits and travels forward as a broad light source. This diffuse light gives 'soft' edges to the shadows and some shadow detail. The quality of the light is similar to that of sunlight through light cloud.

Rodrick Bond

Spotlight

A spotlight can concentrate light at a certain point. The light is directed forward by a hemispherical reflector and focused to a point by a focusing (Fresnel) lens. The shadows will have 'hard' edges with no detail. The quality of the light is similar to direct sunlight. Spotlights can be flooded to give a more diffuse quality. This change from spot to flood is achieved by moving the lamp and the reflector inside the lamp housing away from (spot) or closer to (flood) the lens at the front of the light. On 'full spot' shadows are harsh with no detail, on 'full flood' shadows are softer with some detail. Most spotlights come with barn doors and nets. Barn doors are metal flaps attached to the front of the light and control the shape and amount of light. Nets are pieces of wire gauze of varying densities that reduce the output of the light by diffusing the light at its source without greatly affecting the shadows. They are manufactured in half and one and two stop increments.

Flash

Flash is a generic term referring to an artificial light source of high intensity and short duration. It has a color temperature of 5800K and is balanced to daylight. Unlike tungsten it is not a continuous source of light. Between flashes it has to recycle (recharge) to maximum output before it can be used. Large tungsten lights have an output 100 times greater than the average household light. With a film rated at 100 ISO this will give exposures of around 1/60 second at f4. A modest studio flash with an output of 5000 joules (measurement of output) at the same distance from the subject as the tungsten light will give exposures of around 1/500 second at f11. This is six stops faster or a ratio of 64:1. Its advantage when photographing anything that moves is obvious.

Mick Downes

The advantage of modern flash is its lightweight construction and versatility. Most studio flash systems consist of a power pack, flash heads and attachments. The power pack is usually a separate unit where light output is stored until the instant of exposure. After exposure the power pack recharges ready for the next exposure. Recycling times vary from seconds to fractions of seconds. The faster the recharge to full power the more expensive the unit. The flash heads are the actual light source. The basis of their design is to produce light similar to that produced by floodlights and spotlights. The way in which this is achieved ranges from varying sizes of reflector bowls similar in design to a floodlight to a focusing spotlight equivalent to its tungsten counterpart. Flash, being a non-continuous light source, is generally confined to 'still' photography whereas tungsten lighting is used almost exclusively in 'moving' photography (film, video and TV). However, the lessons learned with one light source apply equally to any other.

Activity 1

Using various resource material compile a collection of studio photographs using tungsten or flash as a light source. Divide into the two categories.

Consider why a particular light source was used, its advantages and differences.

Floodlight

Swimming pool, soft box, fish fryer and others are names for variations of a floodlight. In some the light source is placed inside and to the rear of a collapsible tent with direct light transmitted through a diffuse front surface. In others the light is reflected off a white/silver surface before it is transmitted through a diffuse front surface. These sources create a very soft diffuse light with minimum shadows. Soft diffuse light is also created when flash is used in conjunction with a collapsible umbrella. With umbrellas having a white/silver inside surface, light can be directed into the umbrella and reflected back onto the subject creating a quality of light similar to a soft box. With umbrellas having a transparent diffuse surface light can be directed through the umbrella creating a quality of light less diffuse than the reflected light from the white/silver umbrella.

James Newman

Spotlight

The use of an open flash (direct light to subject without diffusion or reflection) will give the same effect as a spotlight. Some brands have focusing capabilities closely imitating Fresnel spotlights. The light will be hard with no shadow detail. Barn doors, nets and filtration of the light source are approached in exactly the same way as a tungsten source.

Mixed light sources

Any source of light can be combined with another to create interesting lighting effects and shifts in color balance. In a studio situation this can go beyond mixing tungsten with flash and is limited only by one's imagination. Normal domestic lamps are often used as supplementary and practical sources of light. Candles give a warm glow and very soft shadows. Torch light can be used to great effect when painting with light. When working in color do not be afraid to change the color of the light by the use of colored gels over the lights or filtration of the camera. If it gives off light, try using it!

Mixed tungsten and flash - Itti Karuson

Activity 2

Place camera on tripod and attach cable release. Focus on a coin placed on a dark background. Set the shutter speed to T (aperture opens when the shutter is activated and will not close until activated for the second time). Set the aperture to maximum aperture. Darken the studio and open the lens. Using a small torch move its light over the coin as if painting with a brush (large broad strokes) for approximately 10 seconds. This should be done from the camera position. Bracket exposures one stop either side of normal. Repeat this procedure at every f-stop.

Working with studio lights
Common rules

Common rules of physics apply to the use of artificial light sources. When sunlight passes through greater amounts of particles in the atmosphere at dawn or sunset, exposure times increase compared to a reading taken at noon. This applies to clear and overcast days. Exposure times will obviously be shorter on a clear day. Applying these rules to a studio situation, the greater the impedance to the light (diffusion, reflection, filtration) the longer the exposure. In direct light (no diffusion, reflection, filtration) the shorter the exposure.

Another simple rule. The amount of light falling on a subject decreases to 1/4 of its original intensity when the light to subject distance is doubled, and increases by 4x when the light to subject distance is halved. For example, if a reading of f16 is obtained when the light to subject distance is one metre, at two metres the reading would be f8, at four metres f4. These rules do not change regardless of the light source. It is also important to remember contrast in a studio situation is created not only by the reflectance level of the subject matter (SBR) but also by lighting ratios. When referring to lighting ratios the photographer is also referring to lighting contrast. See 'Contrast and Compensation'.

Key light one metre from subject

Key light two metres from subject
- Fabio Sarraff

Activity 3

In a darkened studio place a light one metre from the studio wall and take an incident reading, with the light on, of the light falling upon the wall. Note the reading and move the light on the same axis another one metre away from the wall. Note the reading. Double the distance once more, making a total of four metres. The final reading will be four stops less than the first. What will the distance of the light from the wall have to be to achieve a meter reading of three stops less than the first?

Diffusion

Long before the invention of photography painters had been diffusing light. Light passing through certain materials created a light with soft shadows sympathetic to their subjects. Early writings and drawings of Michelangelo show his studio had a type of cheesecloth hung over the windows. This diffused the harsh sunlight and filled the studio with a soft light more suitable to painting. Any light source can be diffused by placing certain translucent materials between the light source and the subject. This has the effect of diffusing and spreading the light over a greater area by altering the direction of the light waves. Diffusion softens the edges of the shadows and increases shadow detail. At the same time the measured amount of light falling on the subject is decreased. The amount of diffusion is also determined by where the diffusion material is placed in relation to the light source and the subject. The closer the diffusing material to the light source the less diffuse the light. The closer the diffusing material to the subject the more diffuse the light, the softer the edges of the shadows and the greater the shadow detail. There are many diffusion products manufactured specifically for the photographic market. These are products such as scrim, nets, and silks. Other suitable materials are tracing paper, cheesecloth, and window netting provided they are non-flammable or heat-proof.

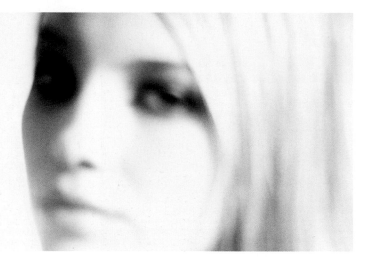

Diffuse light - Kata Bayer

Activity 4

In a darkened studio light a semi-reflective object (e.g. a tomato) with an open flash or tungsten spotlight. Place the light approximately 1.5 metres from the subject.
Observe the source of light reflected in the object and lack of shadow detail.
Diffuse the light source with tracing paper (60cm x 60cm) 50cm from the light.
Observe the apparent increase in the size and diffusion of the light source as reflected in the subject, diffusion of the shadows and increase in shadow detail.
Without moving the light place the tracing paper as close to the subject as possible.
The light source has now become the size of the piece of tracing paper. There will be a soft spread of light over most of the subject with the shadow being almost non-existent.

Reflection

Reflected light is most often used as a way of lighting areas the dominant light source (key light) cannot reach. An example is the strong shadow created by a spotlight when it is to one side of the subject. To obtain detail in the shadow area light has to be reflected into the shadows. This is called fill light and is achieved by collecting direct light from the light source and redirecting it with a reflector. Reflectors can be any size, from a very small mirror to large polystyrene sheets measuring 3m x 1.5m.

Reflected light can also be used as the key light. When photographing a reflective object, or a very diffuse (soft) lighting effect is required, the light source can be directed into a reflector. The reflector becomes the light source and no direct light from the light source is directed at or reflected in the subject. When photographing cars in an exterior situation the car is usually positioned so sunrise or sunset is behind the car. With the sun below the horizon, the sky above and in front of the car is acting as a giant reflector. This is one approach to lighting cars and reflective objects in a studio.

There are many reflective products available manufactured specifically for the photographic market. Other more readily available materials are white card, gray card, colored card, silver foil, aluminium foil, and mirrors.

Reflector as light source - Rodrick Bond

Activity 5

Light a person's face with open flash or tungsten spotlight from behind and to one side.

Observe the deep shadows falling across most of the face.

Using a reflector (white card 1m x 1m) redirect the light into the shadow areas.

Observe how the intensity of the light changes as the reflector is moved closer to and further away from the face.

Expose image at the desired intensity of fill.

Cover the reflector with aluminium foil and repeat the above activity.

Label and keep results for future reference.

Filtration

Filters alter the quality of light by selectively transmitting certain colors or by changing the way light is transmitted. A red filter only transmits red light. A blue filter only transmits blue light and so on. A soft focus filter changes the direction of the light waves in the same way as diffusion material softens a light source. Correction filters alter the color temperature of the light to make it compatible with the film being used. Neutral density filters reduce the amount of light, and therefore exposure, from a light source without affecting its color temperature. Glass, plastic and gelatin filters are used for filtration of the camera lens but gelatin filters are used more often in the filtration of the light source. The advantage of filtering the light source is that different filters can be used on each of the lights whereas with filtering the camera all light entering the lens will be subjected to a common filter. Filters used upon a light source are made of heat-resistant colored gels manufactured to specific safety requirements and color balance. The effect of filtration is obvious and immediate. When working with correctly color balanced lights and camera combined with 'correct' exposure 'what you see is what you get'. When using color filtration with black and white capture a simple way of remembering the effect of a certain filter is that it will lighten its own color and darken all others. Filtration of the camera is normally used for color correction of the entire image. This may be caused by the light source being incompatible with the camera's pre-set color balance or to remove an excess of one color inherent in the light source. However, when capturing Raw file images it is possible to undertake color correction in post-production. See 'Characteristics of Light'.

Polarizing filters are valuable in the control of unwanted reflections and increased color saturation. This is because of their ability to selectively transmit certain wavelengths as they are rotated in front of the camera lens or light source. A wide range of 'effect filters' such as graduated and star burst are also available for on-camera use and post-production software. They can produce some interesting results but should not be used as a substitute for the lack of an original idea or solution to a photographic problem. With camera filtration some exposure compensation may be needed.

Mixed lighting on location - Tracey Hayes

Lighting ratios

Light meters are often incorrectly called exposure meters. Exposure is only one part of its function. It can also be used for measuring lighting ratios. This is achieved by taking an incident reading of the light source from the subject. The meter is pointed at a specific light source to measure the amount of light falling on the subject. If there is more than one light source each light can be measured independently by ensuring only one light source is on at any one time. In this way the ratios between the light sources can be measured.

Lighting ratios and their relationship to SBR and latitude are best demonstrated and understood at a practical level. Take, for example, a photographer using a capture medium known to have a latitude of five stops. To make use of this information the photographer would try to light the subject to within this range. A five stop latitude would allow a photographer to use a maximum lighting ratio of 32:1 (5 stops). This ratio would retain detail in the highlights and the shadows.

Example 1

In a darkened studio a person is lit with a single light source from the right-hand side at 90 degrees to the subject. An incident light meter reading is taken from the right-hand side of the person's face directly towards the light source. The aperture is f45 at 1 second. An incident light meter reading is taken from the left-hand side of the person's face directly towards the opposite side of the studio to where the light is placed. The aperture is f4 at a shutter speed of 1 second. This is a lighting ratio of 128:1 (7 stops).

To reduce this ratio another light or a reflector (fill) is placed on the left-hand side of the subject. The fill is moved towards or away from the subject until an aperture reading no more than three stops lower in number than that from the main light source (f16) is obtained. This is now a lighting ratio of 8:1.

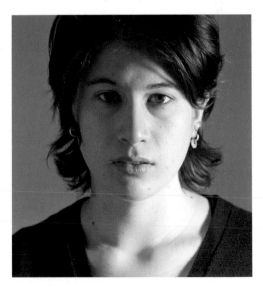

128:1   *8:1*

Example 2

The task is to light three sides of a single colored box with a one stop ratio between each of the sides. Pointing a light meter in the general direction of the subject would give an average reflected reading for 'correct' exposure but would not indicate the difference in the light falling on each of the three sides. This can be achieved by taking either a reflected reading of each side or for a more precise measurement taking an incident reading of each of the three light sources. This would give a measure of the actual amount of light falling on the subject. This information can then be used to adjust the balance of the lights to achieve the required lighting ratio.

1. Spotlight   *2. Spotlight + floodlight*   *3. Spot, flood + reflector*

1. A point source (spotlight) is aimed at the top of a neutral gray box from behind the subject. The shadow falls forward of the subject. An incident reading is taken of the light source by pointing the invercone directly at the spotlight. The reading is f16.

2. A diffuse source (floodlight) is aimed at the left side of the box, ensuring no light affects the top or right side of the box. An incident reading is taken of the floodlight (shield the invercone with your hand to prevent light from the spotlight affecting the reading) by pointing the invercone directly at the floodlight. The reading is f11. This is a lighting ratio between the top and left-hand sides of 2:1 (1 stop).

3. A piece of white card is used to reflect light back into the right-hand side of the box. The light reflected is gathered from the spotlight and floodlight. With both lights on, an incident reading is taken of the reflected light by pointing the invercone directly at the piece of white card. The reading is f8. This is a lighting ratio between the left and right sides of 2:1 (1 stop), and an overall lighting ratio between the top and left-hand side of 4:1 (2 stops).

An incident reading is taken by pointing the invercone from the front of the box back towards the camera. It should be f11. This is an average of the lighting ratio.

For more examples of lighting still life see *Essential Skills: Studio Photography.*

Example 3

The task is to photograph a chain and a paper clip on a textured background. The lighting ratio between the most intense area of the background and the subject should be 8:1. The subject should be in focus, the background out of focus. The approach taken is the same as in Example 2, using incident light meter readings to control lighting ratios and exposure.

James Newman

Using a point source (key light) from the right and above the subject light the staple and chain to create highlights along their top edge. Take an incident reading from the subject to the light source (e.g. f16). Place a diffuse light source (fill light) to the left of the subject. Between this light and the subject place a large sheet of tracing paper (the further the tracing paper is from the light source the more diffuse the light). With the key light turned off take an incident reading from the subject to the diffuse light source. Move the light closer to or further away from the subject until a lighting ratio of 2:1 is achieved (e.g. f11).

Position background approximately one metre behind the staple and chain. Adjust the position of the key light to ensure no shadows from the chain fall on the background. Turn off key light and fill. Place a point source of light behind and to the right of the subject. Aim the light across the background to increase the texture of its surface. Adjust the light until the desired highlights are achieved. Take a reflected reading of the most intense highlight on the background. Adjust this reading by three stops to render the highlight white (e.g. f22 to f11). Move the light closer to or further away from the background until a reading equal to the average of the key light and fill is achieved (e.g. average of f16 and f11 = f11.5). Turn on key light and fill. Filter lights and/or camera for effect. Take an incident reading from the subject to the camera. Choose an exposure aperture with sufficient depth of field to retain focus on the staple and chain but not on the background.

Example 4

A photographer has to create a mid key portrait containing a predominance of average tones but with no extreme highlights or shadows. The result is achieved using a large, diffuse light source, creating a soft, even lighting quality, combined with selective fill and overexposure by one stop to obtain correct skin tones. This is one of the most commonly used forms of portraiture lighting. It is a relatively simple approach to lighting the human form compared to high and low key lighting and will generally produce good results with most subjects. It does, however, lack drama and mood and would not enhance subjects with strong individual character, delicacy of form or great physique.

1. Soft box   *2. Soft box + fill*   *3. Soft box + fill + back light*

1. Place the subject approximately two metres from a large diffusion screen (background). As viewed from the camera place a soft diffuse light source (flash soft box) in front of and to the left of the subject. Place a diffusion screen larger than the light source between the light source and the subject. The screen should be approximately one third of the distance from the light to the subject. Take an incident light meter reading from the subject to the camera. A typical reading would be f11 at 1/250 second.

2. Place a large (2m x 3m) white reflector in front of and to the camera right side of the subject. This will reflect light from the key light source back onto the right side of the subject. Adjust the distance of the reflector from the subject until an incident light meter reading from the subject to the reflector is one stop less than the key light. This should be f8 at 1/250 second. This is a lighting ratio of 2:1 between the left and right sides of the face and when used for exposure will overexpose the left side of the face to reduce any skin imperfections.

3. Place behind the diffusion screen in the background a large diffuse light source (flash soft box). Direct the light through the diffusion screen straight back at the camera. Adjust the light source so an incident light meter reading taken from the subject to the background diffusion screen is two stops more than the incident reading of the subject to camera (f8 at 1/250 second). This background reading should be f16 at 1/250 second. If the subject exposure is set to f8 at 1/250 second the background will appear white.

For more examples of portraiture lighting see *Essential Skills: Studio Photography*.

On location

Studio lights should not be limited to the studio. They can be used on location in conjunction with ambient and existing daylight. With color correction of the light source and/or camera most light sources can produce acceptable and interesting results. Raw file images can be color corrected in post-production. See 'Characteristics of Light'.

Exterior location

Common examples of studio lighting used on location are the images seen in film and television. The same approach can be taken to still images. Artificial light, whether flash or tungsten, is normally used to supplement the existing light present, usually daylight. In this situation correct color is achieved by balancing the camera to daylight (5500K) and filtering the tungsten light source/sources (3200K) with an 80A lighting gel. When using studio flash on location no filtration is required as the color temperature of the flash is equal to average daylight (5500K).

Mixed light

Mixing the color temperature of the light sources can give a more 'natural' look. Despite the fact the human eye corrects all light sources to what appears to be white light, it is visually accepted, and in most cases to great effect, that when we view images created using mixed light sources there should be a difference between the color temperature of the various sources of light within the frame.

Balanced daylight and flash - Tracey Hayes

Interior location

There can be many different light sources with varying color temperatures confronting the photographer on location. This can range from industrial lighting to the glow from a TV. The possibilities and variations are many but the problems they pose can be either corrected with filtration or white balance adjustment to render 'correct' color, or ignored and the differences in color temperature exploited and used to effect.

Daylight balance

In an exterior location all light sources are balanced to the predominance of daylight (5500K). With an interior location (for example, a furnished room with large windows) there can be a mixture of various light sources. Balancing to daylight (5500K) without filtration of the tungsten light sources (3200K) would make the image appear quite different. Daylight in the image would appear 'correct' but any tungsten light source whether artificially introduced (studio) or practical (normal domestic lighting, desk lamps, candles, etc.) would create a warm glow at its source and on subject matter predominantly lit by it. The overall effect would be of white light through the windows, and depending upon the lighting ratio created between the tungsten light and the ambient daylight, an overall warm cast to the image.

Tungsten balance

If the camera is balanced to tungsten (3200K) without filtration of either the daylight (5500K) or the tungsten light sources (3200K) the result would appear different again. Daylight in the image would appear to have a blue cast and any tungsten light source would appear 'correct'. The overall effect would be of blue light through the windows, and depending upon the lighting ratio created between the tungsten light and the ambient daylight, a balance of 'correct' color within the room. It should be remembered filtration of the camera to match the dominant light source would also produce similar results. However, filtration of the camera removes the possibility of selectively filtering the various light sources and color temperatures available to the photographer to create an interesting mix of colors within the frame.

For more examples of lighting on location see *Essential Skills: Studio Photography*.

Domestic tungsten light and daylight - James Newman

Example 5

A designer commissions a photograph of a kitchen. As it is in a residential building the owner has requested the minimum amount of disturbance. The client has requested the lighting enhances the space and balances ambient interior and exterior daylight. The photographer decides upon one exposure, balancing the exterior, interior and introduced lighting. The camera is balanced to daylight. Exterior daylight will be overexposed to reduce the orange/red color cast of domestic tungsten lighting.

Ambient light - daylight and tungsten - incident - 1 sec. @ f8.5

Umbrella flash in hallway balanced to f8.5

Fill flash off ceiling balanced to f8 - John Hay

James Newman

Chris Mollison

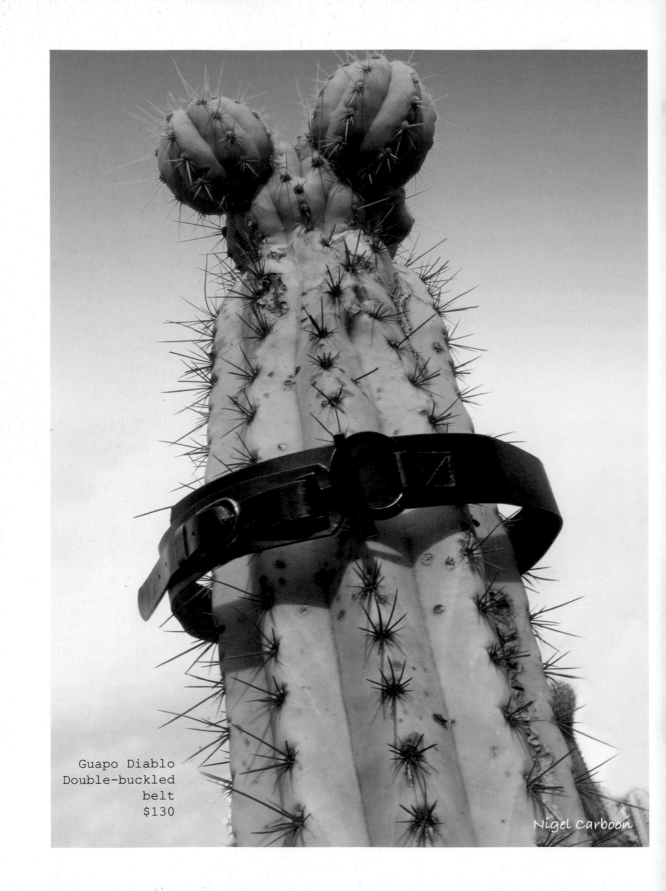

Guapo Diablo
Double-buckled
belt
$130

Nigel Carboon

creative techniques

Daniel Tückmantel

essential skills

~ Develop knowledge and understanding of how light can change the character and mood of subject matter.

~ Develop skills in controlling lighting to achieve creative effect.

~ Observe the use of creative techniques in the production of photographic images.

~ Study an extensive collection of images utilizing creative lighting techniques.

~ Produce photographic images demonstrating a practical understanding

Introduction

The choice, arrangement and design of a subject within the frame determines the effectiveness of its communication. Communication can be increased by having a better understanding of the camera and its controls. Careful consideration is advised when using technical effects. Images are about communication and content and not about technique. Technique should never dominate the image.

Exposure compensation

Exposure compensation is used to correct tonal values that would otherwise have recorded as too dark or too light. It is also used to record detail in highlights or shadows when the brightness range of the subject is high. Exposure compensation can also be used for creative effect. The creative process of photography sometimes requires an exposure that is not correct to produce the desired result. The degree of compensation is only limited by the photographer's imagination and the limitations of the film or image sensor. Interesting results can be achieved by purposely underexposing or overexposing regardless of SBR. Underexposure should be carried out in Adobe Camera Raw and not in camera when using a digital camera.

Mark Galer

Silhouettes

An image described as a silhouette is the dark shadow or outline of the subject against a lighter background. A silhouette can be created by backlighting the subject and reducing the exposure sufficiently to remove detail from the subject. Reducing the exposure by approximately two to three stops is usually required to record the subject as black (this can be achieved in Adobe Camera Raw when using the Raw file format).

Backlighting

A subject is back lit when the dominant light is from behind the subject. To take a reflected reading of the subject from the camera would give an incorrect exposure. A reflected reading of the subject only or an incident reading from the subject to the camera would give correct exposure. The dominance of the backlight can therefore be controlled by exposure compensation.

Haloes

With subjects having an extreme contrast either as a result of SBR or lighting ratios, exposing for the shadow areas will create the effect of massively overexposing the highlights. On its own or combined with lens filtration (soft filter) the result, especially when using a strong backlight, is a halo effect around the subject.

Color saturation

Decreasing exposure by 1/3 or 2/3 of a stop will increase color saturation when capturing with film. The Vibrance slider in Adobe Camera Raw should be used when shooting in the Raw file format using a digital camera. The technique works well in flat midday light. Images can look underexposed when recording tones of known value.

Nigel Carboon

Activity 1

Create the effect of a halo using a dominant backlight and exposure compensation.
Repeat the procedure to create two silhouettes with an interesting profile. One silhouette should have a white or clear background, the second the colors of an evening sky.
Bracket the reduced exposure compensation.
Label the results of each image.

Low key

A low key image is where the dark tones dominate the photograph. Small bright highlights punctuate the shadow areas creating the characteristic mood of a low key image. The position of the light source for a typical low key image is behind the subject or behind and off to one side, so that the deep shadows are created. Appropriate exposure usually centres around how far the exposure can be reduced before the highlights appear dull. The shadow areas are usually devoid of detail when this action is taken unless a certain amount of fill is provided.

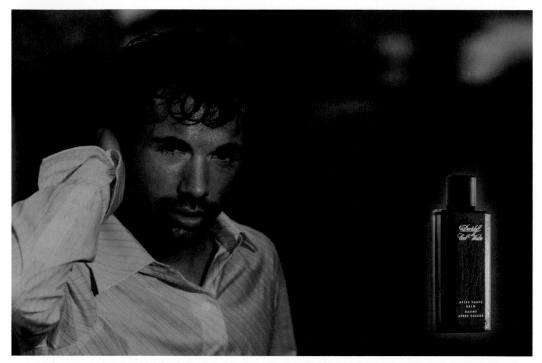

Martin Reftel

High key

A high key image is where light tones dominate. Dark tones are eliminated or reduced by careful choice of the tonal range of the subject matter. Soft diffused lighting from a broad expansive light source is used to reduce shadows. Backgrounds may be flooded with light so that little detail is seen. Increased exposure ensures the tones are predominantly light. Hard edges and fine detail may be reduced by the use of a soft focus filter. A bright background placed close to the subject may also soften the outline of the form. The main light source to illuminate the subject can be provided by skylight, window light or light reflected off a large bright surface. Backgrounds can be overexposed by sunlight.

Activity 2

Create one high key and one low key image.

Describe the lighting used for each image including a record of the indicated exposure and degree of compensation.

Illusion of movement

Closely associated with an understanding of the use of light is the use of the camera to create the illusion of movement. By combining the movement of either the camera, subject or lights, the illusion of movement within a still frame can be created. Using tungsten light in a darkened studio and with the camera lens open, walking slowly through frame (the camera's field of view) will result in a blurred image where you were moving and still image where you stopped. Another way to create movement is to increase exposure time to the longest possible with the light source you are using and move the camera during all or part of the exposure. This is easily achieved with a zoom lens, but also achievable by panning or tilting the camera mounted on a tripod. There are other advantages to using a slow shutter speed when using a combination of flash and tungsten. If the output of the modelling lamps, or supplementary tungsten lighting, is high enough to equal the exposure aperture of the flash output a slower exposure time can be used for the tungsten light than required for the flash. This would allow correct exposure of the flash (which is regulated by aperture and not time) and correct exposure of the tungsten (which is regulated by a combination of aperture and time). This would give the effect when balanced to daylight of a warm afterglow to any object moving before or after the flash exposure.

Itti Karuson

Activity 3

In a darkened studio light a person with a diffuse light source close to camera.
Set the shutter to the longest exposure time relative to the exposure aperture.
With the lens open ask the subject to walk across frame. Vary the speed and rhythm of the movement. Observe the images and compile results.

Mark Galer

Creative post-production

Many creative photographs are not the product of a single exposure but the result of several exposures, which when combined create an abstract or realistic outcome. To create a realistic outcome the photographer must carefully consider the post-production techniques that can be utilized when preparing to capture the component images. Lighting must be of a consistent quality, color temperature and direction throughout the component images and the shadows of a subject must be considered as these will need to be rendered realistically if the final outcome is to be believable. All too often a photographer will carefully capture the subject only to forget to pay attention to the subject's shadow.

Preserving the original shadow in a montage

If all of the subject's shadow is captured and the shadow falls over a smooth surface, it can be preserved in post-production and placed over the new background using the 'Multiply' blend mode. This post-production technique provides photographers burdened with a meticulous eye a useful way of retaining and transplanting subtle and complex shadows. Observe the subtle shadow cast by the leaf in the illustration above. The primary reason for not being able to use this technique is when the shadow falls over a surface that has a different texture to the one in the new location.

Mark Galer

Creating a shadow

If it is not possible to preserve the original shadow of the subject, due to the fact that it is falling over a different surface texture to the new host image, then the photographer could consider taking the following action. Capturing a second image of the subject from the direction of the light source will allow the photographer to create a more accurate shadow than simply using the outline of the subject as seen from the camera angle. This second image can be used as a resource shape for the subject's shadow when the montage is assembled in the image-editing software.

Activity 4

Create a composite image or 'montage' where the subject casts a shadow over its new background. Use either one of the two post-production techniques outlined here to create the final result.

Original image of Lake Rotoiti in New Zealand's South Island (courtesy of John Hay)

Changing the weather in post-production

For some commercial photographers making good photographs even more memorable using Photoshop is all part of the creative process, whilst most photojournalists and documentary photographers, on the other hand, are not allowed this creative freedom. The question 'When does a photograph stop being a photograph?' is one that each photographer must answer for themselves, as photographic images have been manipulated since the very early days of photography and photographers have always been very divided on the answer.

The commercial studio photographer is able to control the quality and direction of light to create the precise mood in order to meet the requirements of the brief. On location, however, the photographer is at the mercy of the weather and the limitations of time (budget). Photoshop is able to lend some assistance to manipulate the mood so that the final image aligns more closely with the requirements of the client and still meets the specified budget. In the illustration above we can perhaps only begin to imagine what it might have looked like as the shafts of light penetrated the morning mist over the still waters with their mirror-like reflections of the distant mountains, but it is possible in post-production to attempt to wind back the clock so that the photographer can recapture the mood, mist and tranquillity of the dawn shot. In post-production the distant mountains were copied and pasted on a new layer. The Transform and Warp commands were then used to perfect the reflection (simulated reflections are rarely as simple as just flipping a copy layer so the Warp Tool was used to massage the reflection into shape). A combination of adjustment layers and the Shadow/Highlight adjustment features was then used to change the color and contrast so that the light emulated the soft light of dawn. The introduction of morning mist and some subtle shafts of warm light complete the picture of tranquility.

Mark Galer

Creating shafts of light

Creating effective landscape images is not exactly rocket science. Choose a beautiful landscape just after dawn, or just before sunset, and add dramatic natural lighting to create emotive and memorable landscape images. Clear blue skies are great for holidays on the beach but the best natural lighting for photography is provided by broken or filtered sunlight through partial cloud cover. Some feel the most memorable of all lighting is when shafts of light break through the clouds. Finding partial cloud cover when the sun is low is relatively easy; being present when shafts of light flood your selected vista, however, can be an elusive and rare event. This final and quintessential ingredient requires patience, persistence and good fortune - or a good helping of post-production editing courtesy of Photoshop. It is possible to add the artificial drama to photographs by selectively lightening an image using an adjustment layer and painting into the adjustment layer mask to restrict the lightening to just certain areas. Creating a custom gradient with soft-edged stripes can be used to effectively create shafts of light. The Free Transform command can then be applied to the mask to make the light seemingly radiate out from its source.

Activity 5

Change the mood or drama of an image in post-production by changing the hue, saturation and brightness of selected areas of the image. Keep a copy of the original image for comparison.

Comment on whether you feel the image appears realistic and what could be improved to increase its sense of realism.

Original Venice image by Craig Shell (sky by Mark Galer)

Changing the sky to change the mood

The sky is an essential ingredient of any memorable landscape image. Unfortunately it is not something the photographer can control unless we have limitless time and patience. The commercial photographer is often required to deliver the goods on a day that suits the client rather than the photographer and weather forecast. In these instances it is worth building a personal stock library of impressive skies that can be utilized to turn ordinary images with bland skies into impressive ones. The digital compact set to a low ISO is ideal for capturing these fleeting moments. The most useful skies to collect are the ones that include detail close to the horizon line, i.e. captured without interference from busy urban skylines, such as can be found at the beach or in the desert. In most cases the sky must be adapted to fit the landscape so the montage is not immediately obvious. In the illustration above the new sky was made brighter as it approached the horizon line and also behind the buildings on the left side of the image to imitate the setting sun.

Paulina Hyrniewiecka

Composite lighting

The lighting of a studio set is often compromised by either limitations of time or the complexity of the lighting that is required for the creative outcome. Take, for instance, the example above, where the ideal lighting required for the creative shadow and the wine is different. Perfect the lighting for one and the quality of the other is compromised. The solution is remarkably simple of course. Perfect the lighting for one at a time and then create a composite image in post-production. The drama of the shadow is created by the use of a spotlight from the side, whereas the wine and label are lit with softer floodlights from the front and rear. Prior to CS3, pin-registering each exposure in-camera using a sturdy tripod was an essential requirement for the success of this technique. Small differences in camera position (such as knocking the tripod between exposures) can now be corrected using the new Auto-Align Layers command.

Imaginative creations - making the impossible appear real

Photoshop is mostly used by amateur photographers to fix images as a result of poor camera or lighting craft. There are, however, times when Photoshop is used as a tool by skilled practitioners to create images that cannot be captured in a single frame taken by the camera. In the component images of this montage (above left) we can see that the photographer has spent a great deal of time in pre-production assessing how to assemble this image in post-production. Unlike some of the images on the previous pages the light and the shadows cannot be simulated entirely in post-production. The photographer has therefore introduced the light in one of the component images during the capture of the still life (physically placing an electric light in the glass container). The model and the jar have been photographed against a black background to enable a higher quality extraction so they can be seamlessly placed in the composite image (black, when placed in the 'Screen' blend mode in Photoshop, is neutral or 'invisible').

Activity 6

Create a composite image changing the light quality for each component image.
Combine elements from each image using post-production software such as Photoshop.
Place the camera on a tripod or use the auto-align feature in the full version of Photoshop to align the component images.

Daniel Tückmantel

The professional montage and retouching techniques, outlined in these activities, are explained in greater detail in Photoshop CS3: Essential Skills *and* Adobe Photoshop Elements Maximum Performance. *These books come with all of the images used in the projects together with supporting movie tutorials.*

Itti Karuson

Daniel Willmott

Tracey Hayes

lighting

assignments

Itti Karuson

essential skills

~ Develop, extend and apply your knowledge and understanding of studio and location lighting, color correction and camera technique.

~ Develop, extend and apply your knowledge and understanding of the practical use of light to create contrast, dimension, mood.

~ Increase your creative ability to interpret a written brief within specific guidelines.

~ Through further study, observation and pre-production understand the resources and skills required to produce high quality photographic images.

~ Produce a series of images to the highest standard fulfilling the assignment criteria plus personal creative interpretation.

Introduction

The assignments in this study guide should be attempted after successful completion of the activities in the previous study guides. Creative interpretation of the written brief is strongly encouraged. Assignments should be completed at an individual level in any order. Allowance should be made for the fact that each assignment may need photographing more than once before a satisfactory result is achieved. Special attention should be taken of the medium in which the photograph is to be used. This will determine image format and in some cases composition. See *Essential Skills: Studio Photography (Art Direction)*.

Tim Barker

This series of images should portray an understanding of what lighting and camera technique can achieve in changing the photographer's perception of the subject and previsualization of the image. Avoid placing a subject on or against a background, taking a normal viewpoint and perspective and lighting for correct color and exposure. This is no different to documentation of the subject. As creative photographic illustrators much more is required. Experiment with viewpoint and lighting. Do not let reality get in the way of creative composition. Perspective, depth, dimension can all be altered to suit the design of the image. The camera will 'see' and record anything you want it to. This does not have to relate to human perception. Separate subjects from the background. Dispense with the concept of backgrounds altogether. The area behind and around the subject is only limited by your imagination. Previsualize, experiment and create.

1. Still life

Subject of your choice photographed at an interior location, making use of filtration and the available ambient light. Any window and practical tungsten light source (desk lamp, etc.) should appear in the photograph. To be used for a single-page color advertisement.

2. Formal portrait

Subject of your choice photographed on location (exterior or interior) making use of artificial tungsten light or studio flash. Horizontal format suitable for exhibition.

3. Time of day

Recreate in the studio an exterior photograph of a typical coffee restaurant table setting. The time of day is either early morning (breakfast menu) or late afternoon. Use color filtration of the light source (flash or tungsten) to achieve the color balance appropriate to the time of day. To be used for single-page color editorial.

4. Available light

A still life of a vase of flowers photographed on location (interior or exterior) using only the available light. It should be photographed in the style of an impressionist painting. Format and capture medium appropriate to the subject matter and desired effect.

5. Crowded street

A series of photographs of a single person in a crowded street to highlight the fact they are different to everyone else. Use should be made of a long focal length lens, selective focus and ambient light. Color double-page spread.

6. Environmental portrait

A series of environmental portraits of people at work, rest or play for an international confectionery manufacturer. The people must be young, from various ethnic backgrounds and must always appear to be enjoying themselves. Use a mixture of available and supplementary lighting. Color point of sale.

7. Product shot

Studio product shot to complement the previous series of portraits. The product should be obvious, yet sympathetic to the mood created by the portraits. Color image.

8. Torchlight

Using torchlight only, light a subject of your choice in the studio or on location. Experiment with exposure and filtration, if required, to achieve a satisfactory result.

Nigel Carboon

Itti Karuson

Glossary

1K	1000 watts, measure of light output.
2K	2000 watts, measure of light output.
5K	5000 watts, measure of light output.
10K	10,000 watts, measure of light output.
12K	12,000 watts, measure of light output.
120	Film format.
2¼	2¼ x 2¼˝. Camera format.
35mm	Camera and film format (24 x 36mm).
500W	500 watts, measure of light output.
5 x 4	5 x 4˝, camera and film format.
6 x 4.5	6 x 4.5cm camera format.
6 x 6	6 x 6cm camera format.
6 x 7	6 x 7cm camera format.
6 x 8	6 x 8cm camera format.
6 x 9	6 x 9cm camera format.
10 x 8	10 x 8 inches camera and film format.
80A	Conversion filter, daylight film to 3200K light source.
80B	Conversion filter, daylight film to 3400K light source.
85B	Conversion filter, tungsten film to daylight.
ACR	Adobe Camera Raw.
AC discharge	5600K continuous light source.
Adobe RGB	A color space that is appropriate for images destined for print output devices that have a larger gamut than sRGB.
Ambient	Available or existing light.
Analyse	To examine in detail.
Aperture	Lens opening controlling intensity of light entering camera.
Arri 650W	Arriflex 650 watt light source (3200K).
ASA	Film speed rating - American Standards Association.
Aspect ratio	The ratio of height to width.
Auto focus	Automatic focusing system, mainly small-format cameras.
Available	Ambient or existing light.
B	Shutter speed setting for exposures in excess of 1 second.
B/g	Background.
Background	Area behind main subject matter.
Backlight	Light source directed at the subject from behind.
Backlit	A subject illuminated from behind.
Balance	A harmonious relationship between elements within the frame.
Banding	Visible steps of tone or color in the final image due to a lack of tonal information in a digital image file.

Barn doors	Metal shutters attached to light source.
Bellows	Lightproof material between front and rear standards.
Bellows extension	When length of bellows exceeds focal length of lens.
Bellows formula	Mathematical process to allow for loss of light.
Bit depth	Number of bits (memory) assigned to recording color or tonal information.
Blurred	Unsharp image, caused by inaccurate focus, shallow depth of field, slow shutter speed, camera vibration or subject movement.
Bounce	Reflected light.
Bracketing	Overexposure and underexposure either side of MIE.
C stands	Vertical stand with adjustable arm.
C-41	Negative film process.
Cable release	Device to release shutter, reduces camera vibration.
Calibration	Adjusting a device such as a computer monitor to a known and repeatable state that is considered standard within the industry.
Camera	Image capturing device.
Camera Raw	Unprocessed image data from a camera's image sensor.
Camera shake	Blurred image caused by camera vibration during exposure.
CCD	Charged Coupled Device. A solid state image pick-up device (sensor or chip) used in digital capture.
Clipping	Loss of detail due to overexposure, underexposure or excessive saturation.
Close down	Decrease in aperture size.
Closest point of focus	Minimum distance at which sharp focus is obtained.
CMOS	Complementary Metal Oxide Semiconductor. A type of image sensor.
Color balance	Photoshop adjustment feature for correcting a color cast in a digital image file.
ColorChecker	A reference card of colors and tones manufactured by Gretag Macbeth.
Color conversion	Use of filtration to balance film to light source.
Color correction	Use of filtration to balance film to light source.
Color management	The process of maintaining the accuracy of colors from the capture device to the output device.
Color profile	Information that describes the unique color characteristics of a device such as a scanner, camera, monitor or printer.
Color space	An accurately defined range of colors which may be a smaller portion of the human vision.
Color temperature	Measure of the relationship between light source and film.
Compensation	Variation in exposure from MIE to obtain appropriate exposure.
Complementary	Color - see 'Primary' and 'Secondary'.
Compound	In lens design, indicating use of multiple optical elements.
Compression	Underdevelopment allowing a high-contrast subject brightness range to be recorded on film. See 'The Zone System'.
Concept	Idea or meaning.
Context	Circumstances relevant to subject under consideration.
Continuous tone	A smooth transition of color or tone without a visible dots or bands.

Contrast	The difference in brightness between the darkest and lightest areas of the image or subject.
Cord	Electrical lead.
Covering power	Ability of a lens to cover film format with an image.
CPU	Central Processing Unit of a camera used to compute exposure.
Cropping	Alter image format to enhance composition.
Cut-off	Loss of image due to camera aberrations.
Cutter	Device used to control spread and direction of light.
Cyclorama	Visually seamless studio.
Darkcloth	Material used to give a clearer image on ground glass.
Dark slide	Cut film holder.
Daylight	5500K.
Dedicated flash	Flash regulated by camera's exposure meter.
Dense	Overexposed negative, underexposed positive.
Density	Measure of the opacity of tone on a negative.
Depth of field	Area of sharpness variable by aperture or focal length.
Depth of focus	Distance through which the film plane moves without losing focus.
Design	Basis of visual composition.
Diagonal	A line neither horizontal nor vertical.
Diaphragm	Aperture.
Differential focusing	Use of focus to highlight subject areas.
Diffuse	Dispersion of light (spread out) and not focused.
Diffuser	Material used to disperse light.
Digital	Images recorded in the form of binary numbers.
Digital image	Computer generated image created with pixels, not film.
Digital Negative	Adobe's open source Raw file format.
DIN	Film speed rating - Deutsche Industrie Norm.
Dioptres	Close-up lenses.
Direct light	Light direct from source to subject without interference.
Distortion	Lens aberration or apparent change in perspective.
DNG	Adobe's Digital Negative format.
Double dark slide	Cut film holder.
Dynamic	Visual energy.
DX coding	Bar coded film rating.
E-6	Transparency film process.
Ecu	Extreme close-up.
Electronic flash	Mobile 5800K light source of high intensity and short duration.
Emulsion	Light-sensitive coating on film or paper.
Equivalent	Combinations of aperture and time producing equal exposure.
EV	Numerical values used in exposure evaluation without reference to aperture or time.
Evaluate	Estimate the value or quality of a piece of work.

Expansion	Manipulating the separation of zones in B & W processing.
Exposing right	Increasing exposure when using a digital camera to increase the quality of shadow information.
Exposure	Combined effect of intensity and duration of light on light-sensitive material.
Exposure compensation	The action increasing or decreasing exposure from a meter-indicated exposure to obtain an appropriate exposure.
Exposure factor	Indication of the increase in light required to obtain correct exposure.
Exposure meter	Device for the measurement of light.
Exposure value	Numerical values used in exposure evaluation without reference to aperture or time.
Extreme contrast	Subject brightness range that exceeds the film or sensor's ability to record all detail.
F-stop	Numerical system indicating aperture diameter.
Fall	A movement on large-format camera front and rear standards.
Fast film	Film with high ISO, can be used with low light levels.
Field of view	Area visible through the camera's viewing system.
Figure and ground	Relationship between subject and background.
Fill	Use of light to increase detail in shadow area.
Fill flash	Flash used to lower the subject brightness range.
Film	Imaging medium.
Film speed	Rating of film's sensitivity to light.
Filter	Optical device used to modify transmitted light.
Filter factor	Number indicating the effect of the filter's density on exposure.
Flare	Unwanted light entering the camera and falling on film plane.
Flash	Mobile 5800K light source, high intensity, short duration.
Floodlight	Diffuse tungsten light source.
Focal	Term used to describe optical situations.
Focal length	Lens to image distance when focused at infinity.
Focal plane	Where the film will receive exposure.
Focal plane shutter	Shutter mechanism next to film plane.
Focal point	Point of focus at the film plane or point of interest in the image.
Focusing	Creating a sharp image by adjustment of the lens to film distance.
Fog/fogging	Effect of light upon unexposed film.
Foreground	Area in front of subject matter.
Format	Camera size, image area or orientation of camera.
Frame	Boundary of composed area.
Fresnel	Glass lens used in spotlight.
Front light	Light from camera to subject.
Front standard	Front section of large-format camera.

Gamma | A mathematical formula describing the relationship between the input and output of a device. The Gamma setting on a monitor and in Photoshop controls the mid-tone brightness.

Gels | Color filters used on light sources.

Genre | Style or category of photography.

Gobos | Shaped cutters placed in front of light source.

Grain | Particles of metallic silver or dye which make up the film image.

Gray card | Contrast and exposure reference, reflects 18% of light.

Grayscale | An image where the color values have been converted to tones of gray.

Ground glass | Viewing and focusing screen of large-format camera.

Guide number | Measurement of flash power relative to ISO and flash to subject distance.

Halftone | Commercial printing process, reproduces tone using a pattern of dots printed by offset litho.

Hard/harsh light | Directional light with defined shadows.

HDR | High Dynamic Range.

High Dynamic Range | An image with full detail in the darkest shadows and brightest highlights that has been created from a subject with a brightness range that exceeds the latitude of the capture device. The HDR image is assembled in the image-editing software using multiple exposures.

High key | Dominant light tones and highlight densities.

Highlight | Area of subject giving highest exposure value.

Histogram | A graphical representation of a digital image indicating the pixels allocated to each level of brightness.

Hot shoe | Mounting position for on-camera flash.

HSL | Hue, Saturation and Luminance. Color controls found in Adobe Camera Raw and Photoshop Lightroom.

Hue | The name of a color, e.g. red, green or blue.

Hyperfocal distance | Nearest distance in focus when lens is set to infinity.

Image sensor | Light-sensitive digital chip used in digital cameras.

Incandescent | Tungsten light source.

Incident | Light meter reading from subject to camera using a diffuser (invercone).

Infinity | Point of focus where bellows extension equals focal length.

Infrared film | A film sensitive to wavelengths of light longer than 720nm invisible to the human eye.

Invercone | Trademark of Weston. Dome-shaped diffuser used for incident light meter readings.

Inverse square law | Mathematical formula for measuring the fall-off (reduced intensity) of light over a given distance.

Iris | Aperture/diaphragm.

ISO | Film speed rating - International Standards Organization.

JPEG (.jpg)	Joint Photographic Experts Group. Popular image compression file format used for images destined for the World Wide Web.
Key light	Main light source relative to lighting ratio.
Laboratory	Film processing facility.
Landscape	Horizontal format.
Large format	5 x 4 inch camera, 10 x 8 inch camera.
Latitude	Ability of the film or image sensor to record the brightness range of the subject.
Lens	Optical device used to bring an image to focus at the film plane.
Lens angle	Angle of lens to subject.
Lens cut-off	Inadequate covering power.
Lens hood	Device to stop excess light entering the lens.
Light	The essence of photography.
Lightbox	Transparency viewing system.
Lighting contrast	Difference between highlights and shadows.
Lighting grid	Studio overhead lighting system.
Lighting ratio	Balance and relationship between light falling on subject.
Light meter	Device for the measurement of light.
Long lens	Lens with a reduced field of view compared to normal.
Loupe	Viewing lens.
Low key	Dominant dark tones and shadow densities.
Luminance range	Range of light intensity falling on subject.
M	Flash synchronization setting for flash bulbs.
Macro	Extreme close-up.
Matrix metering	Reflected meter reading averaged from segments within the image area. Preprogrammed bias given to differing segments.
Maximum aperture	Largest lens opening, smallest f-stop.
Medium format	2¼ inch or 6cm film or image sensor size.
Meter	Light meter.
MIE	Meter-Indicated Exposure.
Minimum aperture	Smallest lens opening, largest f-stop.
Monorail	Support mechanism for large-format camera.
Multiple exposure	More than one exposure on the same piece of film.
ND	Neutral Density filter.
Negative	Film medium with reversed tones.
Negatives	Exposed, processed negative film.
Neutral density	Filter to reduce exposure without affecting color.
Noise	Electronic interference producing speckles within the image.
Non-cord	Flash not requiring direct connection to shutter.
Normal lens	Perspective and angle of view approximately equivalent to the human eye.

Objective	Factual and non-subjective analysis of information.
Opaque	Does not transmit light.
Open up	Increase lens aperture size.
Orthochromatic	Film which is only sensitive to blue and green light.
Out of gamut	Beyond the range of colors that a particular device can capture, display or print.
Overall focus	Image where everything appears sharp.
Overdevelopment	When manufacturer's processing recommendations have been exceeded.
Overexposure	Exposure greater than meter-indicated exposure.
Panchromatic	Film which is sensitive to blue, green and red light.
Panning	Camera follows moving subject during exposure.
Perspective	The illusion of depth and distance in two dimensions. The relationship between near and far imaged objects.
Photoflood	3400K tungsten light source.
Photograph	Image created by the action of light and chemistry.
Plane	Focal plane.
Polarizing filter	A filter used to remove polarized light.
Portrait	Type of photograph or vertical image format.
Positive	Transparency.
Posterization	Visible steps of tone or color in the final image due to a lack of tonal information in a digital image file.
Post-production	Modifications made to an image after the initial capture using image-editing software such as Adobe Camera Raw or Photoshop.
P.o.v.	Point of view.
Preview	Observing image at exposure aperture.
Previsualize	The ability to decide what the photographic image will look like before the exposure.
Primary colors	The basic colors used to create all other colors. The colors blue, green and red are the additive primaries while cyan, magenta and yellow are the subtractive primaries.
Process	Development of exposed film.
Profile	A record of the unique characteristics of how a device records, displays or prints color and tone.
ProPhoto RGB	The largest of the working spaces used in Photoshop.
Pull	Under-processing of film.
Push	Over-processing of film.
QI	Quartz Iodine light source.

Raw	The unprocessed data recorded by a digital image sensor. Sometimes referred to as Camera Raw or the 'digital negative'.
Rear standard	Rear section of large-format camera.
Reciprocity failure	Inability of film to behave predictably at exposure extremes.
Reflectance	Amount of light from a reflective surface.
Reflectance range	Subject contrast measured in even light.
Reflected	Light coming from a reflective surface.
Reflection	Specular image from a reflective surface.
Reflector	Material used to reflect light.
Refraction	Deviation of light.
Resolution	Optical measure of definition, also called sharpness.
Reversal	Color transparency film.
Rim light	Outline around a subject created by a light source.
Rise	A movement on large-format camera front and rear standard.
Saturation	Intensity or richness of color.
SBR	Subject Brightness Range, a measurement of subject contrast.
Scale	Size relationship within subject matter.
Scrim	Diffusing material.
Secondary	Complementary to primary colors, yellow, magenta, cyan.
Selective focus	Use of focus and depth of field to emphasize subject areas.
Shadow	Unlit area within the image.
Sharp	In focus.
Shutter	Device controlling the duration (time) of exposure.
Shutter priority	Semi-automatic exposure mode. The photographer selects the shutter and the camera sets the aperture automatically.
Shutter speed	Specific time selected for correct exposure.
Side light	Light from side to subject.
Silhouette	Object with no detail against background with detail.
Slave	Remote firing system for multiple flash heads.
Slide	Transparency usually 24 x 36mm.
Slow film	Film with reduced sensitivity and low ISO rating.
SLR	Single Lens Reflex camera; viewfinder image is identical to image captured by film or image sensor.
Small format	35mm film or a digital camera with a sensor no larger than 35mm.
Snoot	Cone-shaped device to control the spread of light.
Softbox	Heavily diffuse light source.
Soft light	Diffuse light source with ill-defined shadows.
Specular	Highly reflective surfaces.
Specular highlight	The brightest tone in an image that is not absolute white (255 or paper white).
Speed	ISO rating, exposure time relative to shutter speed.
Spotlight	Light source controlled by optical manipulation of a focusing lens.
Spot meter	Reflective light meter capable of reading small selected areas.

sRGB	A working space closely aligned to the color space of a typical monitor.
Standard lens	Perspective and angle of view equivalent to the eye.
Stock	Chosen film emulsion.
Stop	Selected lens aperture relative to exposure.
Stop down	Decrease in aperture size.
Strobe	5800K light source.
Studio	Photographic workplace.
Subject	Main emphasis within image area.
Subjective	Interpretative and non-objective analysis of information.
Subject reflectance	Amount of light reflected from the subject.
Swing	A movement on large-format front or rear standards.
Symmetrical	Image balance and visual harmony.
Sync	Flash synchronization.
Sync lead	Cable used to synchronize flash.
Sync speed	Shutter speed designated to flash.
T	Shutter speed setting for exposures in excess of 1 second.
T-stop	Calibration of light actually transmitted by a lens.
Text	Printed word.
Thin	Overexposed positive, underexposed negative.
Thyristor	Electronic switch used to control electronic flash discharge.
TIFF	Tagged Image File Format. Popular digital image file format for desktop publishing applications.
Tilt	A movement on large-format front or rear standards.
Time	Shutter speed, measure of duration of light.
Time exposure	Exposure greater than 1 second.
Tonal range	Difference between highlights and shadows.
Tone	A tint of color or shade of gray.
Trace	Material used to diffuse light.
Transmitted light	Light that passes through another medium.
Transparency	Positive film image.
Transparent	Allowing light to pass through.
Tripod	Camera support.
Tripod clamp	Device used to connect camera to tripod.
TTL	Through-The-Lens light metering system.
Tungsten	3200K light source.
Typeface	Size and style of type.
Typography	Selection of typeface.
Underdevelopment	When manufacturer's processing recommendations have been reduced.
Uprating film	Increasing the film speed.
UV	Ultraviolet radiation invisible to the human vision.

Vertical	At right angles to the horizontal plane.
Vibrance slider	A control for increasing color saturation in Adobe Camera Raw or Photoshop Lightroom. This control is less likely to render colors out of gamut when compared to the Saturation slider.
Viewpoint	Camera to subject position.
Visualize	Ability to exercise visual imagination.
White balance	The process of setting a neutral white point or value as the color temperature that is illuminating the subject changes.
White point	The color of white that a device creates, displays or prints.
Wide angle	Lens with a greater field of view than normal.
Workflow	A term used to describe a sequence of steps to achieve a particular result.
Working space	A color space that is optimized for editing images in a product such as Adobe Photoshop.
XMP	eXtensible Metadata Platform. Data saved with an image file.
X-synch.	Synchronization setting for electronic flash.
X-synch. socket	Co-axial socket on lens or camera for external flash cable.
Zone System	Exposure system related to tonal values.

Index